USING
COMMON W
Times and
All Saints to Ca.   ıas
A Practical Guide

David Kennedy
Introduction by John Sweet

CHURCH HOUSE
PUBLISHING

Church House Publishing
Church House
Great Smith Street
London SW1P 3NZ
Telephone   020 7898 1451
Fax   020 7898 1449

ISBN   978–0–7151–2309-6

Published 2006 by Church House Publishing

Typeset in   11pt Sabon and 11.5pt Gill Sans
              by RefineCatch Ltd, Bungay, Suffolk

Printed by   MPG Books Ltd, Bodmin, Cornwall

Contents

	Foreword by the Rt Revd Stephen Platten	iv
	Introduction by John Sweet	1
1	A banquet of word and worship	13
2	All Saints to Advent	19
	Seasonal material	24
	All Saints' Day	26
	All Souls' Day	44
	Remembrance Sunday	52
	Christ the King	54
3	Advent	57
	Seasonal material	62
	Advent carol services	64
	The Advent Wreath	65
	Advent Antiphons	72
	The Advent Prose	73
	Christmas in Advent	74
	'Darkness to light' imagery	76
4	Christmas Season	78
	Seasonal material	82
	The Eucharist of Christmas Night or Morning	84
	Carol services in the Christmas Season	87
	Christingle services and crib services	89
	Additional prayers for use at Christmastide	91
	Resource material for the beginning of a new year	92
	Common Worship: Festivals	94
5	Epiphany Season	98
	Seasonal material	101
	Seasonal material connected with the theme of Unity	102
	Seasonal material connected with the theme of Mission	105
	The Eucharist on the Feast of the Epiphany	106
	The Eucharist on the Festival of the Baptism of Christ	109
	A Service for the Festival of the Baptism of Christ	111
	The Eucharist on the Feast of the Presentation of Christ in the Temple	113
6	Conclusion	118
	Index	120

Foreword

In this past generation there has been nothing less than a revolution in worship patterns in the Church of England. The treasury that is *The Book of Common Prayer* remains our wellspring, but *Common Worship* has helped us better appreciate the contrasts afforded by the seasons of the Church's year. This has allowed churches to engage flexibly with local needs within and beyond their congregations.

Times and Seasons offers a rich banquet. This *Using Common Worship: Times and Seasons* volume will help those who plan and lead worship to provide a balanced yet imaginative diet from within this banquet. As the Liturgical Commission shifts its focus to the formation of God's people through worship, so the *Using Common Worship* series of books offers a set of invaluable tools for the planning and leading of worship.

Both *Times and Seasons* and this 'companion', then, allow for an effective and imaginative engagement with the tradition of the Church. That broad stream of tradition includes both the best of Anglican worship and spirituality together with a blending of ancient sources and contemporary patterns. These newly honed tools will give the Church the opportunity to offer a still better 'sacrifice of praise and thanksgiving' to God in Jesus Christ our Lord.

✠ *Stephen Wakefield*
Chairman of the Liturgical Commission

Introduction
John Sweet

The publication in 1986 of *Lent, Holy Week and Easter*, and taking part in the services it inspired, opened up a new dimension in worship for many Anglicans and others. The experience of the traditional services for Maundy Thursday, Good Friday and the Easter Vigil transformed the Easter Season. In his introduction the Liturgical Commission's Chairman wrote:

> Our worship is one with the worship of the whole Church of the ages. To be a Christian is to enter into the tradition consciously and gladly. Our task has been to distil from the experience of the past the forms appropriate to the present and to present them in the idioms of the present . . . to preserve the proper continuity with the past, but with freshness.

They were offering not texts to be followed slavishly but a directory to choose from sensitively and imaginatively.

In 1991 the Commission produced *The Promise of His Glory*, drawing equally imaginatively on traditional materials to enrich worship in the period from All Saints to Candlemas: presenting Advent as a season of joyful expectancy, Christmas and Epiphany as celebrating the whole Incarnation, not just the Nativity, and Candlemas as the hinge or pivot, ending the 40 days of Christmas and pointing forward in Simeon's second oracle to the Passion.

People joked that what was now needed was *Pentecost to Michaelmas*. In 1993 Michael Perham, one of the architects of the Commission's two books, produced *Enriching the Christian Year*, to give greater depth to services for Holy Days and commemorations, and for themes like Creation or Justice and Peace.

These three books were designed for use with the *Alternative Service Book 1980*, then the only authorized liturgy alongside *The Book of Common Prayer*. With the advent of *Common Worship* in 2000 it became necessary to replace these books, drawing out their strengths and making provision where new needs were seen, under the title *Times and Seasons*. This present book offers practical guidance in using this rich material for the period All Saints to Candlemas.

How much more enrichment, one may ask, can the average congregation stomach? Is this journey really necessary? Part of the answer might be that since the Reformation our Anglican diet has in most places been wholesome but plain. Some Protestants thought the Church had departed from the pure New Testament pattern – 'the great apostasy from the Apostles' time to this' – and so dropped accretions to Scripture in their worship, but Anglicans and Lutherans, though pruning out much, did not drop the Church's Year and the Saints altogether. The Bible became central, but the biblical understanding of time and place, which was second nature to the early Christian world, gradually faded; poetry gave way to literal fact. The poetry of the Church's Year was still strong in the seventeenth-century divines, who were nurtured in the Fathers, and it resurfaced in the nineteenth-century Anglo-Catholic revival. But this enrichment of worship, the recovery of colour, light and movement, aroused suspicion and alarm, and to the Church at large, apart from Christmas and Easter, the Church's Year meant little. For most people Lent was merely a season of self-denial, and Advent, where it was observed, was of the same flavour. So, returning to the present, if the riches of *Times and Seasons* are to be digestible and nourishing, it may help to see how time and place figure in the poetic logic of the Bible (about which, see below).

Another justification of this work might be that, where worship had been largely didactic and morally edifying, the recovery of symbolism, poetry, colour and movement has been, to many, enlarging and joyful, and in our ecumenical climate the riches of the other traditions can be welcomed.

On the other hand, another consideration may be suspicion of set forms of prayer and worship; extempore prayers may seem truer to the gospel freedom of the Spirit. But is not today's language, on the lips of many of us, sadly in need of enrichment? The banks of material that *Times and Seasons* gives us to draw on are not to be used slavishly. They can inspire our own free praying and our service planning as worship leaders.

The choice of Scripture readings is an important part of the *Times and Seasons* provision, and there may be a similar question mark against lectionaries, official patterns of readings for the Church's Year: do they put a strait-jacket on God's Word, dictating from the centre what we need on the ground for our local situation? But may not local leaders impose their own strait-jacket? Most of us, left to ourselves, have our canon within the canon. A pattern arising out of long ecumenical consultation, like the triennial *Revised Common Lectionary*, may cover Scripture more comprehensively and constructively, as well as uniting worshippers across the world in what they hear; congregations, like people, are not self-sufficient individuals but all members of the Body. The triennial Sunday lectionary has another plus: it allows us to hear Matthew, Mark and Luke not homogenized, but each in his own voice.

Local needs may always override. *Times and Seasons* does not dictate but provides a frame or context within which regular weekly worship can take on new depth and meaning.

The seasons

All Saints

All Saints' Day celebrates men and women in whose lives the Church as a whole has seen the grace of God powerfully at work. In the early days it was the cult of martyrs that flourished. Many were unrecorded and so unhonoured, whereas places like Antioch and Rome had more known martyrs than there were days of the year, so a common feast of all martyrs was instituted. It was observed on Easter Friday in Syria in the fifth century, and on the octave of Pentecost in the Byzantine Liturgy. In Rome it was kept on 13 May as the feast of All Martyrs and All Saints and Our Lady. This link with the Easter season and Christ's victory was lost sight of when the Roman feast of 13 May was transferred to 1 November, with the title All Saints. This date does, however, allow a link forward to the Advent themes of the Day of the Lord, death, judgement, heaven, and hell, followed as it is on 2 November by All Souls, the Commemoration of the Faithful Departed.

This sequence of All Saints and All Souls does raise questions. First, for St Paul, all Christians are 'saints' or 'called to be saints', set apart to be holy. Reserving the term for outstanding Christians, good though it is to celebrate what God has done in them, is in danger of obscuring

God's work in all Christians, known and unknown. Secondly, praying for the departed. Paul was confident that 'God who began the good work in you will bring it to completion by the day of Jesus Christ' (Philippians 1.6). He expected this to come very soon, but as time went on and life continued it was natural to pray for all Christians *in via*, on the way, living and departed, that God's work might be completed in them.

From very early times there was a general commemoration in the Eucharist of all the Christian dead, not just martyrs or otherwise distinguished, and the date of the present observance is due to Odilo of Cluny in about AD 1000. Since the Reformation many Anglicans have been sensitive about praying for the Christian dead, as calling in question the finality of Christ's redemption. But this is to miss the both-and of the New Testament paradox: we are already justified and glorified (Romans 8.1, 30) *and* must appear before the judgement seat of Christ to answer for our deeds (2 Corinthians 5.10). Theologically, a common mind on the propriety of such prayer has been emerging; as the Introduction to this season in *Times and Seasons* puts it: 'Redemption is a work of God's grace; it is God who redeems us in Christ and there is nothing to be done beyond what Christ has done. But we still wait for the final consummation of God's new creation in Christ.' It is natural to think prayerfully of what remains to be done in us, and in all *in via*, before we can see God in peace. The introduction continues,

> We also sense that it is a fearful thing to come before the unutterable goodness and holiness of God, even for those who are redeemed in Christ; that it is searing as well as life-giving to experience God's mercy; and this instinct also is expressed in the liturgy of All Souls' Day. (*Times and Seasons*, p. 537)

In the run up to Advent, *Common Worship* has departed from the *ASB* pattern of nine Sundays before Christmas. All Saints' Sunday is followed by Remembrance Sunday, and finally comes the Sunday of Christ the King (a feast instituted by Pope Pius XI in 1925, to celebrate the all-embracing authority of Christ and encourage us to seek his peace). It celebrates not his actual Ascension enthronement but its meaning for a world in the aftermath of war (see 'on point and line' below), in the dark days of the year (for us in the north) when we prepare to celebrate the victory of light over darkness.

The year that begins with the hope of the coming Messiah ends with the proclamation of his universal sovereignty . . . final judgement is one of his kingly purposes. The Feast of Christ the King returns us to the Advent themes of judgement, with which the cycle once more begins. (*Times and Seasons*, p. 537)

Advent

The Latin *adventus* means 'coming' or 'arrival', translating the Greek *parousia*, which can also mean 'presence'; it normally refers to Christ's final coming or manifestation. In the Greek world *parousia* was a technical term for the king's arrival at a city to hold assize, to punish criminals and honour the deserving. Citizens would come out to meet him in their best clothes, with joyful hymns of welcome. In Paul's picture, 'we will be caught up in the clouds . . . to meet the Lord in the air' (1 Thessalonians 4.17). This theme of meeting, the union of God with humanity, of heaven with earth, is one of the deep structures of the Christian Year; it will surface again in the Greek title for Candlemas, *hypapante*, meeting.

Advent as a season emerged in the West as a preparation for the festival of the Nativity. In Gaul in the fifth century it was a penitential season of six Sundays, echoing the six Sundays of Lent. In Spain and Italy it was five Sundays, as in the oldest Roman lectionary, and Rome later reduced it to four, which became the norm. (Perhaps there is a trace of the 'five Sunday season' in *The Book of Common Prayer*'s 'Stir up Sunday', the Next before Advent.)

The link with Lent was lost and need not be renewed, for the theme is serious but joyful expectation. We prepare to celebrate Christ's first coming at Bethlehem and his final coming or manifestation in glory as Judge; in the Old Testament a judge sorts things out and puts them to rights, and, as in the Book of Judges, is also a saviour (cf. Philippians 3.20, 21).

In God's time these two comings are one and the same. He 'who was, and is, and is to come' is always the Coming One – the Lord who comes suddenly to his Temple in Malachi (3.1), and on Palm Sunday; the Lord who comes Sunday by Sunday in the Eucharist, in anticipation of his final coming as judge (1 Corinthians 11.26–32). The characteristic Advent prayer is *Maranatha*, 'Our Lord, come', or in the Aramaic it could equally be 'Our Lord is here' (1 Corinthians 16.22; Revelation

22.20, in Greek – both in eucharistic contexts). These layers of reference point us back to the themes of All Saints and All Souls, and forward to Candlemas, Palm Sunday and the Day of the Lord at Calvary. To us the Incarnation is a series of points on a line. In God's time it is one Day; everything is connected with everything else.

Christmas

The historical origin of Christmas is unclear. December 25 was the date of the winter solstice in the West (6 January in the East). The celebration of *natalis solis invicti*, the 'birthday of the unconquered Sun', had been fixed as 25 December in 274, 62 years before the first evidence of the celebration of Christmas in Rome. Constantine encouraged the Church to adapt features of sun worship and built St Peter's on the Vatican Hill, where the sun worship of the Mithras cult already took place.

Was this the Christianization of a pagan festival? It seems more likely that the true clue is the date of Passover (25 March in the West, 6 April in the East) and Jewish identification of end with beginning: seeing the conception of Jesus as one with his Paschal victory and dating his birth nine months later. Such temporal coincidences were commonplace for the Jews, as they were for poets like T. S. Eliot and John Donne (see his poem 'Upon the Annunciation and Passion falling upon one day, 1608').

If this was indeed the historical origin of Christmas, the coincidence of the winter solstice was a providential opportunity to show Christ as fulfilling the festivals of the pagan as well as the Jewish year, as we will see also for Epiphany. *Times and Seasons* suggests taking up the secular observance of New Year, with acclamations like 'Christ is the first and the last, the beginning and the end' – this, with the blessing of the Paschal Candle, is another link between Christmas and Easter and the New Creation.

Epiphany

The celebration on 6 January in the East was described by the pilgrim Egeria in Jerusalem in the fourth century as an eight-day festival (an 'octave') of great magnificence. From other Eastern evidence and from places in the West under Eastern influence, it is clear it was a celebration, not just of the actual birth as originally in Rome, but of God's glory revealed in the events of the Incarnation: the visit of the Magi, the Baptism of Christ, and his first miracle at Cana, when 'he revealed his glory' (John 2.11). The word Epiphany means 'manifestation'.

If the date, as for Christmas in the West, was historically due to the theological linking of Christ's conception and passion rather than to the Christianization of a pagan festival, it is still significant that 6 January in the Greek world was linked with the virgin birth of Dionysus, who was held to reveal his presence on that day by water becoming wine in his temple. Here again is fulfilment: Dionysus represented the spirit that inspired Greek religion and culture, but when men had well drunk, the good wine came with Christ (John 2.10). Likewise the visit of the wise men, as Matthew relates it, is more than the manifestation of Christ to the Gentiles (as in *The Book of Common Prayer*): they were Magi, astrologers, the men of science of the ancient world, paying homage to the true light.

The wedding at Cana inspired nuptial imagery, the marriage of Christ and his Church – the latent theme of meeting and union we find at Advent, in the hymn 'Sleepers, wake!': 'Come forth ye virgins wise; the Bridegroom comes, arise!' – and again at Candlemas. The descent of the Spirit at Christ's baptism was seen as the hallowing of all water; it became one of the occasions when baptism was celebrated publicly in East and West.

It has been a happy insight of modern liturgy to grasp Christmas and Epiphany as together celebrating the whole Incarnation: the 'point' in time of the birth drawn out into the 'line' of Jesus' whole story, with 25 December (or 6 January) hinting at its end at Passover, a hint made clearer in Candlemas at the end of the 40 days season.

Candlemas

In *The Book of Common Prayer* this feast is called the Purification of the Blessed Virgin Mary. In *Common Worship* it is the Presentation of Christ in the Temple, which stems from the story in Luke 2: Jesus' parents visit Jerusalem to present him in the Temple 40 days after his birth in accordance with the Law of the First-born (Exodus 13.1). With this Luke has coalesced the requirement for a woman to be ritually purified after childbirth (Leviticus 12.6). There is an echo also of the story of Hannah presenting Samuel to the Lord for his service (1 Samuel 1.11ff.), a theme applied to us in the collect for the day.

The common title, Candlemas, stems from Simeon's first oracle, hailing Jesus as 'a light to lighten the Gentiles', and from the use of candles throughout the Advent and Christmas seasons to celebrate the True Light. The feast originated in Jerusalem and was celebrated in the Byzantine Church as the *hypapante* (meeting), the meeting of the Old Dispensation and the New in the person of Jesus with his parents and Simeon and Anna; the presence of Anna (omitted in the BCP Gospel for the day) is perhaps a Lukan hint of the partnership of men and women in the ministry of the New Covenant. Meeting, the union of heaven and earth, is a deep theme throughout these seasons.

In the West it was kept as a feast of Mary, whence the BCP title. Simeon's second oracle predicts Israel's rejection of Jesus, its fall and rising again – the sword that will pierce Mary, who represents Israel as mother of the Messiah, as well as human mother of Jesus. It points forward to cross and to resurrection (Jesus' work in raising up fallen Israel). The feast thus closes the Christmas season while pointing ahead to Holy Week and Easter, a hinge or pivot in the Church's Year, another instance of the whole story line encapsulated in a moment. The lovely Durham Cathedral meditation in this book (pp. 114-15) brings out all these themes and more.

Now, a few more detailed reflections on the way time is understood and, by extension, the way liturgical time operates.

Time and place in biblical logic: liturgical time

Point and line

The whole story line of salvation can be concentrated in a moment, 'God's mystery which is Christ in you' (Colossians 1.26–2.3). In every service of word and sacrament we make present the birth, death and resurrection of Jesus and the coming of the Holy Spirit, all in the context of God's plan from before the foundation of the world and his promise to sum up all things in Christ. But there is a limit to what we can inwardly digest in any one moment: the times and seasons of the Christian Year spread out the immeasurable riches of 'God's mystery, that is, Christ himself', so that we can be fed by each part of the story without losing sight of its place in the whole.

The recovery of the Bible at the Reformation was an incalculable gain, but at the cost of largely losing the Christian Year, which had been distorted by accretions and legalism. If we are to recover it with a good conscience we need to remind ourselves of the biblical understanding of time and place, and of the biblical logic familiar to poets but foolishness to the Western scientific world view.

Two ages

There are two overlapping dimensions: ours, which is linear, a line running from Creation to the Last Day, the Day of the Lord; and God's, for whom past, present and future are all one: 'Thy time is now and evermore, Thy place is everywhere' (John Mason, 1645–94). Heaven is not 'a place', it is where God is, and every place can be a meeting place with God (Genesis 28.10–17).

The Jews expressed it as the Two Ages: This (evil) Age – ours – under the control of the 'ruler of this world' and That Age, the Age to Come – God's – which is from before the beginning of the world, and will at the Last Day swallow up this Age into the kingdom of God (like the cows in Pharaoh's dream in reverse). In the Old Testament the Age to Come, heaven, is always impinging – in events like the Exodus and through prophets who stand in God's council and pronounce his words on earth. And humans can keep entering it in worship and prayer: the Temple is the throne-room of heaven itself (Isaiah 6). The day of the Lord is always close, for good or ill. False worship and injustice bring back the chaos to which God gave order in the beginning: darkness and disaster, instead of the blessing Israel expected of the Day of the Lord (Amos 5.18; 8.9). It disrupts the communication, the communion, of heaven and earth. God's final restoration of order (Eden) at the End waits on human obedience, in which worship – rehearsing the mighty acts of God, reminding God – is central. All Jewish theology and worship is 'eschatological', orientated to the End which is (in God's time) also the Beginning, the first day of the New Creation, the new cosmic 'week', so that first day and eighth day are one and the same (thence the liturgical 'octave').

For Christians the climactic Day has come. Calvary *is* the Day of the Lord, when the sun goes down at noon (Amos 8.9; Mark 15.33). Easter

Sunday *is* the first day of the new cosmic 'week', the New Creation. Good Friday and Easter Sunday are theologically one 'day', not two. Christ is the first-fruits of the final harvest of the dead; in biblical thinking the first in a series includes, *is*, the whole: Adam includes all under sin, separation from God; the Second Adam includes all in him, in his risen Body, the Church.

Christians live between the beginning of the End and its final Day of consummation (hence the 'millennium': 'with the Lord one day is as a thousand years', 2 Peter 3.8). It is as if Christ's victory has established a bridgehead of light within the darkness of This Age and we have a foot in both camps. We are citizens of heaven, but are still under Caesar; in the world but not of the world; in the flesh but living not according to the flesh but according to the Spirit. We are amphibians, but need constantly to breathe the heavenly air, for the 'god of this age' is still prowling, terrible, though his time is short (1 Peter 5.8; Revelation 12.12), and God has given us 'the medicine of immortality', in Ignatius of Antioch's phrase, the antidote to the serpent's poison, in the breaking of the one bread. This is the characteristic Christian eschatology: the end is both already and not yet.

Liturgical time

What are separate points on the world's time-line may be one and the same in the heavenly perspective we enter in worship. Each Passover night for Jews does not just re-enact the night God brought Israel out of Egypt, it *is* the night. In biblical logic, remembrance, *anamnesis*, is more than making a mental image of a past event, more than re-enacting it: it brings what is *there*, in God's dimension, into our present and makes it effective (for good or ill: 1 Corinthians 11.26–30). There is 'real presence'.

By the same token the Four Nights of the Easter Vigil in *Times and Seasons* are all 'this night'. The night of the Nativity is the darkness into which God said *Fiat lux*; Christ's birth, his descent into the darkness of this world, is the same as his *descensus ad inferos* (Ephesians 4.9) – and this does not contradict the later picture of his descent into hell to harrow it.

On this understanding, prayer and worship are a joyful entry into God's time, heaven; heaven not as the ideal world of Platonic philosophy, accessed by *gnosis*, knowledge, but as the truly real world where we truly belong. It is, as the Eastern Orthodox hold, 'playing at heaven', and the immeasurable richness of the mystery is played out in a series of moments, each a different facet of the mystery, each encapsulating the whole. It is this world, hidden within our world of the senses, that *Times and Seasons* aims to help us enter and enjoy, and this book is a practical guide to its use.

Some people, offered this new wine, may say (or feel) 'the old is good' (Luke 5.39). Psychologically many are not attuned to this liturgical realism and have no seasonal feeling; for them worship is morally and doctrinally uplifting and edifying; Lent is about self-denial rather than sharing Jesus' journey to Jerusalem with the bitter-sweet taste of Candlemas in our mouths. As St Paul said, some hold certain days as special, others regard all days alike; there must be no condemning or despising, only what builds up the church (Romans 14). Mediterranean Catholics and those outside the western materialist tradition may be more 'amphibious' than Northern Protestants, more open to heaven and to real presence in worship. The poet might say, ' 'Tis ye, 'tis your estrangéd faces / that miss the many-splendoured thing' (Francis Thompson, 'In no strange land').

But the crucial question is not 'is it congenial?' but 'is it true?'. Do we enter heaven in worship? Is there real presence? Or is it imagination, make-believe? Our pragmatic age asks to see concrete effects. We can only say that we walk by faith, not sight. We *believe* in the reality of what we do, a faith shared by Jews, by the Church through the ages, and by poets and dramatists – for as Epiphany hints through the Cana story, Christ fulfils Dionysus as well as Moses. In a one-dimensional age for which the past is forgotten and the future is only the present with more options, our liturgy has a gospel to proclaim: hope of unimaginably glorious transformation and faith that it is fact, already within our grasp.

Worship is what we are made for, and *Times and Seasons* offers resources to enrich our liturgy in a deeply biblical way. For example, the Purification-Presentation feast acts as a hinge not just between Birth and Passion but between Old Covenant and New. It is an enacted statement of Luke's balanced theology: Jesus' parents' respect for the Law of Moses and the expectancy of Simeon and Anna are both 'anti-Marcionite' (that is, against regarding the Old Testament as dead letter) and point forward to the final purification that Jesus achieved and the removal of all impurity and taint from women and those outside the Law. Here is an instance in which liturgy can embody doctrinal truths in an undoctrinaire way, subliminally, through the deep resonances of the rites – *lex orandi lex credendi*! It is one of the means by which, in Pastor Robinson's words to the Pilgrim Fathers, 'God hath much more light and truth to break forth from his Holy Word'.

1 A banquet of word and worship

[N]othing should be spared in trying to make certain that for *all* those who come to Church, nothing less than a banquet of word and worship is carefully prepared for each successive Sunday, or whenever and wherever God's people meet for worship.

Michael Marshall

Banquets are lavish; they are varied and balanced; they require good and careful planning, painstaking preparation, exciting and attractive delivery. Historically, Anglican worship since the Reformation has been marked by a certain simplicity and predictability. Michael Perham has commented that in the Prayer Book, the only difference between the Eucharist for the Epiphany and the Eucharist for Ash Wednesday is the collect, epistle and gospel. In the days before hymnody, there was little seasonal colour. But a positive aspect of the legacy of the Reformation was that the Church of England retained a calendar and, through it, has evolved patterns and styles of worship to celebrate the moods and textures of the seasons, both ecclesiastical and agricultural. Over the last hundred years in particular, through music and hymnody, ceremonial and decoration, and by a long process of liturgical renewal, Anglicanism has embraced diversity and enrichment in its worship. A large part of the motivation for this is the desire to prepare a banquet for the feeding and nurturing of God's people. It is also a sign of engagement with the many-faceted aspects of God's mission, and the fruits of exploring the rich and multi-layered story of redemption. All of this comes together in the celebration of God's love and faithfulness in the theatre of Christian worship.

Times and Seasons is offered to the Church as a directory of resources for clergy, Readers, worship leaders, musicians, intercessors and all who contribute to the renewal of worship in our day. It takes its place among other volumes in the *Common Worship* project, but it is unmistakably a manual from which discerning choices are to be made.

A complementary volume, *Common Worship: Festivals*, is a liturgical book for use on a lectern or holy table; *Times and Seasons* is for use in the study, at home, or wherever Christian worship is planned, prepared for and thought about.

Enrichment

The major characteristic of *Times and Seasons* is the provision of enrichment material for the seasons of the Christian Year. This has been a particular development in liturgical revision in the Church of England over the last century. It began in a very modest way in the 1927/28 Prayer Book with the provision of, for example, seasonal sentences of Scripture for Morning and Evening Prayer, and a wider choice of eucharistic proper prefaces. This continued in the Series 1/ Series 2 families of alternative services. There was further, though still modest, expansion in the Series 3 family of rites, which led to the *ASB*. *Lent, Holy Week and Easter: Services and Prayers*, commended by the House of Bishops, was the first resource book to advertise itself as a 'directory' from which choices could be made, but it concentrated on particular main liturgies rather than seasonal material more generally. The major development came through *Patterns for Worship* (1989, 1995) and *The Promise of His Glory* (1990, 1991), both of which included seasonal resources for both 'one-off' and regular services. This included material where, under *ASB* conventions, 'any suitable words may be used', such as

- introduction to confession

- intercessions

- introduction to the Peace.

This was further developed in the unofficial production, *Enriching the Christian Year* (1993), compiled by Michael Perham with others who had served on the Liturgical Commission. This volume made good some omissions from *Lent, Holy Week and Easter*, and made provision for other parts of the liturgical year not as yet covered by other publications.

Times and Seasons has incorporated, adapted and added to such existing material to provide for each season or occasion:

- a bank of seasonal resources suitable for use at the Eucharist or a Service of the Word;

- some fully worked out services for the major festivals of the Christian year;

- other devotional and liturgical material for occasional use, as determined by the particular traditions and themes associated with each season.

Such resources need to be adapted to the local context in which they will be used. As with other *Common Worship* material, this invites the use of technology in the production of high quality, customized service booklets or the use of PowerPoint and other resources for the projection of texts in worship spaces.

Seasonal material

In general, the resources for each season are set out using the following headings:

- Invitations to confession

- Kyrie confessions

- Gospel acclamations

- Intercessions

- Introductions to the Peace

- Prayers at the Preparation of the Table

- Extended Prefaces

- Short Prefaces

- Blessings and Endings

- Short Passages of Scripture

While most of the above headings are familiar from *The Promise of His Glory, Patterns for Worship, Enriching the Christian Year* and the seasonal material in *Common Worship: Main Volume* (published in 2000 and henceforth cited as *Main Volume*), 'Short Passages of Scripture' is an entirely new section. While *Common Worship* did not follow *ASB* in providing sentences of Scripture in Order 1 Holy Communion, there is, nevertheless, a long tradition of using scriptural sentences in the western liturgical tradition. These 'short passages of Scripture' are not designated for particular points in the liturgy; some will easily commend themselves for use at the Gathering, at the Preparation of the Table or the post-communion, as a response to Bible reading or even as a repeated 'refrain' throughout an act of worship, whether sacramental or a Service of the Word. At the Eucharist, they are *not* intended as 'introductory sentences' as in *ASB*; if used as part of the Gathering, they should follow the liturgical greeting.

Fully worked out services

Times and Seasons has followed *Lent, Holy Week and Easter* and *The Promise of His Glory* in providing some fully worked out services in each section of the book, not as inflexible impositions, but as models for liturgical formation and the establishment of common norms and conventions. Other models are given in *New Patterns for Worship*. These show how seasonal material can be worked into the structure of, for example, Holy Communion Order 1. They also provide for those occasions where annual ceremonies are commonly used, such as the procession of palms on Palm Sunday, the footwashing on Maundy Thursday, or a candle-lit procession on the Presentation of Christ in the Temple. Three *different* patterns are given for the Easter Liturgy.

Devotional and seasonal material for occasional use

From the Advent Wreath to the Way of the Cross, from Thanksgiving for the Holy Ones of God to Stations of the Resurrection, from the Rogation Procession to Christingle services, resources and ideas are provided to supplement the statutory services of Holy Communion, Morning and Evening Prayer and a Service of the Word. These resources can be woven into other acts of worship or developed into new and creative forms of liturgy according to local need.

Setting limits

The guiding principles and rationale behind the inclusion of some aspects and the exclusion of others are fully set out in the Introduction to *Times and Seasons*. Limits of space meant that choices had to be made.

One practical decision was to relocate some material in a separate volume: *Common Worship: Festivals*. This volume is conceived as a book for use in church, providing full sets of resources (technically called 'propers') for the following occasions:

- The Naming and Circumcision of Jesus
- The Conversion of Paul
- Joseph of Nazareth
- The Annunciation of Our Lord to the Blessed Virgin Mary
- The Visit of the Blessed Virgin Mary to Elizabeth
- The Birth of John the Baptist
- Mary Magdalene
- The Transfiguration of Our Lord
- Holy Cross Day
- Michael and All Angels
- The Christmas Saints (Stephen, John, The Holy Innocents)

And individual and group commemorations (called 'commons') of:

- The Blessed Virgin Mary
- Apostles and Evangelists
- Martyrs
- Teachers of the Faith
- Bishops and other Pastors
- Members of Religious Communities
- Missionaries
- Any Saint: Holy Men and Women

The *Festivals* volume will also include collects and Holy Communion Order 1; in other words, all the liturgical resources needed for these celebrations in one book. References to *Festivals* in this book are to the Synod Report (GS 1549).

This guide

This book is the first of two volumes and covers the period from All Saints' Day to Candlemas, the Feast of the Presentation of Christ in the Temple. It therefore includes:

- All Saints to the Eve of Advent Sunday

- Advent

- the Christmas Season

- the Epiphany Season

Volume 2 will cover

- Lent

- Passiontide and Holy Week

- the Easter Liturgy

- the Easter Season

- Trinity to All Saints

- The Agricultural Year

- Embertide

This first volume aims to introduce and expound the resources and services from All Saints to Candlemas, and to make practical suggestions for creative use of this diverse material. It tries to view worship holistically, recognizing that Christian worship is far more than mere texts (although texts are an Anglican preoccupation). Worship embraces Christian people in all their infinite variety and giftedness, places, furnishings, symbols and actions. It uses the moods and atmospheres of the time of day and the seasons of the year. It is formed by its engagement with the Christian story, both in its roots in Judaism and through 2,000 years of Christian history, with its accumulated wisdom, spiritualities, symbols, traditions and cultural insights.

My hope is that this book will stretch imaginations and help local churches to think about the possibilities for worship and that it will assist in preparing the banquet. Bon appetit!

2 All Saints to Advent

Give me the wings of faith to rise
within the veil, and see
the saints above, how great their joys,
how bright their glories be.

Isaac Watts

'Heaven in ordinarie'

The month of November is associated with the onset of winter, shortening days, dark nights, fallen leaves, fog and frost, a declining year. Christianly, it opens with the great and joyful feast of All Saints, which provides a backcloth for this pre-Advent season, even though, technically, we are still in 'ordinary time'. But from celebrating the saints in glory, we quickly turn to remembrance: the Commemoration of the Faithful Departed or All Souls' Day on 2 November; the secular, though still resonant, Bonfire or Fireworks Night on 5 November, followed quickly by Armistice Day and Remembrance Sunday; and the change in gear in the lectionary, which invites us to ponder the 'Last Things', the eschatological tradition in the Scriptures, leading us towards Advent. In many ways, the spirituality is of looking heavenwards, bound up with the ultimate salvation of all the saints of every age and the coming of the kingdom, when, at last, heaven and earth shall be fully one.

Stretching Advent

The Promise of His Glory sought to give this period greater cohesiveness by designating it 'the *kingdom* season'. The idea of 'kingdom' was chosen deliberately to suggest the longing for the final in-breaking of the kingdom of God in judgement and mercy, to which the eschatological passages in Scripture point. As we shall see, the four weeks of Advent and the ever-growing anticipation of Christmas leave scant time for a proper treatment of these significant theological and spiritual themes. Historically, the length of Advent has varied, and most contemporary lectionaries anticipate Advent during these weeks. While formal revision of the calendar through General Synod rejected a 'kingdom season' as such in favour of 'Sundays before Advent', nevertheless the substance of the 'season' remains, a clear gear change is undertaken, symbolized in many churches by the use of red vestments and hangings. The material in *Times and Seasons* provides a distinctive liturgical feel to these days. In many ways, the liturgy reflects the time of year, the sense of encroaching darkness and cold, the strong themes of remembrance and longing for salvation, the very human dialogue between loss and hope, promise and fulfilment. It has rightly been said, that the November material represents an inculturation of our experience with appropriate theological and liturgical themes as we approach the end of the year and recognizes our setting in the northern hemisphere, just as we associate and interpret Easter with the onset of Spring.

Calendar and lectionary

Within the All Saints to Advent season, there are four distinctive celebrations:

- All Saints' Day (1 November or the Sunday between 30 October and 5 November)

- All Souls' Day (2 November)

- Remembrance Sunday (Sunday nearest 11 November)

- Christ the King (Sunday next before Advent)

This illustrates the different rankings in the *Common Worship* calendar:

- All Saints' Day is a Principal Feast

- All Souls' Day is a Lesser Festival

- Christ the King is a Festival

So, in terms of ranking, All Saints' Day is one of the nine great annual celebrations, alongside such days as Christmas Day, Easter Day and Pentecost. Christ the King, as a Festival, is placed alongside the Apostles and Evangelists and such celebrations as The Baptism of Christ and Holy Cross Day. In the case of All Souls, designated as a Lesser Festival in the Calendar, local churches are given discretion whether or not to observe it and at what level. Local 'upgrading' of such festivals is possible, as set out on p. 530 of *Main Volume*.

The period All Saints to Advent has some flexibility. Depending on the day of the week on which All Saints' Day and Christmas Day fall (the latter determining the length of Advent), there may be four or three Sundays before Advent. The collect and lectionary material set for the Fourth Sunday before Advent either anticipates or follows All Saints' Day, or may be observed as All Saints' Sunday, using the 1 November provision, if All Saints is not observed on 1 November. The collect and readings for the Third Sunday before Advent were chosen to complement Remembrance Sunday, and may be used on the Second Sunday before Advent in years when this is the nearest Sunday to 11 November. The Sunday before Advent is always kept as the Feast of Christ the King.

The lectionary for the Principal Service illustrates how eschatological themes, anticipating Advent, begin to emerge. As well as the biblical references, I have provided a short quotation from the passages cited, giving a useful flavour of the themes employed.

Fourth Sunday before Advent

Year A

Micah 3.5–12	Jerusalem shall become a heap of ruins
Psalm 43 *or*	I will go to the altar of God
Psalm 107.1–8	Those the Lord redeemed from the hands of their enemies
1 Thessalonians 2.9–13	God, who calls you into his own kingdom and glory
Matthew 24.1–14	And then the end will come

Year B

Deuteronomy 6.1–9	You shall love the Lord your God
Psalm 119.1–8	Blessed are those whose way is pure
Hebrews 9.11–14	The blood of Christ will purify our conscience from dead works
Mark 12.28–34	You are not far from the kingdom of God

Year C

Isaiah 1.10–18	Though your sins are like scarlet they shall be like snow

Psalm 32.1–8	Happy the one whose transgression is forgiven
2 Thessalonians 1.1–12	When the Lord Jesus is revealed from heaven with his mighty angels
Luke 19.1–10	Today salvation has come to this house

Third Sunday before Advent

Year A

Wisdom 6.12–16 *or*	Wisdom is radiant and unfailing
Amos 5.18–24	Alas for you who desire the day of the Lord!
Wisdom 6.17–20 *or*	The desire for wisdom leads to a kingdom
Psalm 70	Come to me quickly, O God
1 Thessalonians 4.13–18	The Lord himself will descend from heaven
Matthew 25.1–13	The parable of the ten bridesmaids

Year B

Jonah 3.1–5, 10	God changed his mind about the calamity that he said he would bring upon them
Psalm 62.5–12	Wait on God alone in stillness, O my soul
Hebrews 9.24–28	Christ will appear again, to save those who wait eagerly for him
Mark 1.14–20	The kingdom of God has come near

Year C

Job 19.23–27a	I know that my Redeemer lives and that at the last he will stand upon earth
Psalm 17.1–8 (9)	Keep me as the apple of your eye
2 Thessalonians 2.1–5,13–17	As to the coming of our Lord Jesus Christ
Luke 20.27–38	Some Sadducees who say there is no resurrection

Second Sunday before Advent

Year A

Zephaniah 1.7, 12–18	The day of the Lord is at hand
Psalm 90.1–8 (9–11), 12	Teach us to number our days

| 1 Thessalonians 5.1–11 | The day of the Lord will come as a thief in the night |
| Matthew 25.14–30 | The parable of the talents |

Year B

Daniel 12.1–3	Many of those who sleep in the dust of the earth shall awake
Psalm 16	In your presence is the fullness of joy
Hebrews 10.11–14, (15–18), 19–25	All the more as you see the Day approaching
Mark 13.1–8	This is but the beginnings of the birth pangs.

Year C

Malachi 4.1–2a	See, the day is coming, burning like an oven
Psalm 98	In righteousness he shall judge the world
2 Thessalonians 3.6–13	Some of you are living in idleness
Luke 21.5–19	These things must take place, but the end will not follow immediately

Christ the King

Year A

Ezekiel 34.11–16, 20–24	I will set over them one true shepherd, my servant David
Psalm 95.1–7 (8)	The Lord is a great king above all gods
Ephesians 1.15–23	God has put all things under Christ's feet
Matthew 25.31–46	The parable of the sheep and goats

Year B

Daniel 7.9–10, 13–14	I saw one like a human being coming with the clouds of heaven
Psalm 93	The Lord has put on his glory
Revelation 1.4b–8	Look! He is coming with the clouds
John 18.33–37	My kingdom is not from this world

Year C

Jeremiah 23.1–6	I will raise up for David a righteous branch
Psalm 46	I will be exalted among the nations
Colossians 1.11–20	For in him all the fullness of God was pleased to dwell
Luke 23.33–43	'This is the King of the Jews'

23

There is a consistency here, for while the readings for the Fourth Sunday before Advent reflect its proximity to All Saints' Day, they also introduce eschatological and kingdom themes. The readings set for Christ the King are very different from Ascensiontide, for example, when the triumphant enthronement of Christ is celebrated. In the former, the gospel in particular explores the 'darker' side of the kingdom: the parable of the sheep and goats (Year A) and material from the passion narratives (Years B and C). The intervening Sundays are dominated by the Thessalonian letters and eschatological parables and discourses.

Seasonal material

Invitations to confession Three forms are provided. The first, based on Jesus' announcement of the kingdom (Matthew 4.17), is drawn from the seasonal provision in the *Main Volume* for 'the day after All Saints' Day until the day before the First Sunday of Advent'. The second is from *Patterns*, referring to the 'heavenly banquet . . . with all the saints'. The third is the call to confession from the 1968 ecumenical Order for Remembrance Sunday.

Confessions Three forms are given: the first two are 'Kyrie Confessions' and the third a congregational text:

- the first 'Kyrie' form is drawn from *Enriching*, based on verses from Psalm 145, with explicit reference to God's 'faithful servants';

- the second is from David Silk's *In Penitence and Faith*, drawing on Psalm 85;

- the third form, a general confession, is from *Patterns*, adapted from Psalm 51.

Gospel acclamations Of the four forms given, the first is from the *Main Volume* for this season, based on Luke 19.38; the others are drawn from Matthew 5.3, Colossians 1.18 and Luke 21.36 respectively.

Intercessions Three sets are provided:

- the first, from *New Patterns*, incorporates material from Isaiah 61 (cf. the manifesto of Luke 4.16–21) related to the kingdom and is strongly mission focused;

- the second is Ascension based, relating to the kingship of Christ;

- the third is from the Eucharist for All Saints in *Promise*.

Introduction to the Peace Both texts are drawn from the *Main Volume*: the first for this season and the second from the provision for Saints' Days.

Prayer at the Preparation of the Table A new composition:

> To you we come, Father of lights,
> with angels and saints,
> where heaven and earth unite.
> May Jesus meet us in the breaking of the bread.
> **Amen.**

Prefaces Of the two texts, the first is from the *Main Volume*, and the second from *New Patterns*.

> And now we give you thanks
> because in him you have received us as your sons and
>   daughters,
> joined us in one fellowship with the saints,
> and made us citizens of your kingdom.

Extended Preface From the *Main Volume* for this season.

Blessings and Endings Of the three 'short blessing' texts, the first is drawn from the *Main Volume* for this season; the second, from *Enriching*, is a suitable text for All Saints' Day, All Souls or memorial services

> May Christ who makes saints of sinners,
> who has transformed those we remember today,
> raise and strengthen you that he may transform the world;
> and the blessing . . .

and the third is the resonant blessing, first published in the order for All Souls in *Promise*, and now included in the Funeral Service.

> May God give to you and to all those whom you love
> his comfort and his peace, his light and his joy,
> in this world and the next;
> and the blessing . . .

The extended (or solemn) tripartite blessing is drawn from the *President's Edition*, and a short acclamation, based on 1 Chronicles 12.11, is from *New Patterns*.

Short Passages of Scripture Nine such texts are given: the first two are clearly introductory; the rest may be used at various points in the liturgy.

All Saints' Day

As All Saints' Day is a Principal Feast in the *Common Worship* Calendar, it may be observed in a number of ways:

- on 1 November alone;

- on 1 November *and* on the Sunday between 30 October and 5 November;

- on the Sunday between 30 October and 5 November kept as All Saints' Sunday.

The lectionary provides sets of readings to cover all three possibilities. The aim is to enable Christian churches to make the most of a very important festival.

In the New Testament, the word 'saint' is used of all Christians (see Romans 1.7), but in Christian history it became used with a capital 'S' for heroes and heroines of the faith duly canonized under Roman Catholic procedures. Since the Reformation, the Church of England has had no machinery for canonization, but has included particular exemplars of 'virtuous and godly living' in successive calendars. The feast of All Saints embraces both the heroes/heroines and the countless millions of faithful Christians who have served Christ in their several generations. The feast is a great celebration of the Church triumphant, and expression of the unity of all God's people living and departed.

The Eucharist of All Saints

Times and Seasons has incorporated a number of fully worked out services, following *Lent, Holy Week and Easter, The Promise of His Glory* and the specimen services in *New Patterns for Worship*. This is not intended to impose on the Church a particular form of seasonal liturgy or to limit local creativity. Rather, it provides models for liturgical formation, and suggests some common texts for the principal celebrations of the Christian Year. The Eucharist for All Saints conforms to the structure of Holy Communion Order 1, and suggests seasonal texts where appropriate. The following points are noteworthy:

- At the Greeting an exhortation may be used which brings out the festal nature of the celebration:

> Rejoice, people of God, praise the Lord!
> Let us keep the feast in honour of all God's saints,
> in whose victory the angels rejoice and glorify the Son of
>   God.

- In place of Gloria in excelsis, the Beatitudes may be said or sung (this may appropriately be done throughout the pre-Advent season), or metrical versions such as 'Blest are the pure in heart' may be used.

- The Prayer at the Preparation of the Table is from *Main Volume* and adapts an ancient prayer from *The Didache*, an early church manual.

- A seasonal invitation to communion is suggested:

> I heard the voice of a great multitude crying, Alleluia!
> The Lord our God has entered into his kingdom.
> **Blessed are those who are called to the supper of**
>   **the Lamb.**

- An alternative Dismissal is provided, with acclamation and short gospel reading.

Dismissal Gospels

A new and distinctive feature of *Times and Seasons* is the provision for 'dismissal Gospels'. This is an attempt to develop the spirituality of being 'sent out' as God's people. As the post-communion prayer in Order 1 says:

> **Send us out**
> **in the power of your Spirit**
> **to live and work**
> **to your praise and glory. Amen.**

So the proclamation of a short Gospel reading immediately before the blessing and liturgical dismissal strengthens the sense that as a church we are called to *live* the gospel and so to participate in Christ's ongoing mission and service to the world he has redeemed.

While this is a new feature in contemporary Anglican worship, it is in fact a recovery of a much older tradition. In the medieval period it was the custom to say or sing 'the last Gospel' at the end of the mass, usually but not exclusively John 1.1–14. While in this context the reading was more devotional than mission-orientated, nevertheless liturgical renewal is often a case of breathing new life into old traditions and ceremonies.

Dismissal Gospels may be proclaimed from the lectern or, in a Eucharist, by a minister at or near the altar. Or they may be proclaimed from the back of the church, possibly from the font area or near the principal door of the church. Where possible and practical, the whole congregation can move during the final hymn to the place of dismissal; this emphasizes the church as a pilgrim people and brings out the inherent drama in the liturgy.

'The Alternative Dismissal for the Feast of All Saints' incorporates an acclamation, dismissal Gospel, blessing and dismissal.

After the post-communion prayer(s):

> **Acclamation**
>
> Great is the Lord and greatly to be praised:
> **there is no end of his greatness.**
>
> One generation shall praise your works to another
> **and shall declare your power.**

All your works praise you, Lord,
and your faithful servants bless you.

They make known the glory of your kingdom
and speak of your power.

My mouth shall speak the praise of the Lord:
let everything bless his holy name for ever and ever.

The Dismissal Gospel

Hear the gospel of our Lord Jesus Christ according to John.
Glory to you, O Lord.

[Jesus said,] 'I have made your name known to those you gave
me from the world. They were yours, and you gave them to me,
and they have kept your word. Now they know that everything
you have given me is from you; for the words that you gave to
me I have given to them, and they have received them and
know in truth that I came from you; and they have believed that
you sent me. I am asking on their behalf; I am not asking on
behalf of the world, but on behalf of those whom you gave me,
because they are yours.'   *John 17. 6–9*

At the end the reader says

This is the Gospel of the Lord.
Praise to you, O Christ.

Blessing

May God,
who kindled the fire of his love in the hearts of the saints,
pour upon you the riches of his grace.
Amen.

May he give you joy in their fellowship
and a share in their praises.
Amen.

May he strengthen you to follow them in the way of holiness
and to come to the full radiance of glory.
Amen.

And the blessing . . .

The Dismissal

Following God's saints in the ways of holiness and truth,
go in the peace of Christ.
Thanks be to God.

All Saints' Church celebrated its patronal festival on 1 November
with a splendid Sung Eucharist, using the Eucharist for All Saints
material in *T & S*. Churches in the Deanery were all invited along,
there was a long procession of clergy and Readers, acolytes and
servers. There was much ceremonial with the use of incense.
The small regular choir was augmented with members of the
congregation and the local Choral Society; they sang a Latin
setting of the mass and two motets. The service was followed by a
party and fireworks. On the following Sunday, the Vicar and PCC
decided to hold a Service of the Word as an accessible form of
service to which people on the fringe of the church could be invited.
They started with the structure on p. 24 of the *Main Volume*:

¶ A Service of the Word

Preparation

The minister welcomes the people with the **Greeting**.
Authorized Prayers of Penitence may be used here
   or in the **Prayers**.
The Venite, Kyries, Gloria, a hymn, song, or a set of
   responses may be used.
The **Collect** is said either here or in the **Prayers**.

The Liturgy of the Word

This includes
¶ **readings (or a reading) from Holy Scripture**
¶ a **psalm**, or, if occasion demands, a scriptural song
¶ a **sermon**
¶ an **authorized Creed**, or, if occasion demands,
   an **authorized Affirmation of Faith**.

Prayers

These include
¶ **intercessions and thanksgivings**

¶ **the Lord's Prayer**

Conclusion

The service concludes with a **blessing, dismissal** or other **liturgical ending**.

They then 'clothed' the structure as follows:

Preparation

Greeting

President   Praise God! For the Lord our God the almighty reigns!
All   **Let us rejoice and be glad and give him the glory.**
                                                New Patterns A27

We stand before the throne of God
with countless crowds
from every nation and race, tribe and language.
Blessing and glory and wisdom,
thanksgiving and honour, power and might
be to our God for ever and ever.
Amen.   *New Patterns A24*

The Lord be with you
and also with you.

Hymn

Prayers of Penitence

Minister   Jesus says, 'Repent, for the kingdom of heaven is close
           at hand'. So let us turn away from sin and turn to
           Christ, confessing our sins in penitence and faith.
                                       T&S All Saints to Advent

Silence is kept.

All   Lord God,
           we have sinned against you;
           we have done evil in your sight.
           We are sorry and repent.
           Have mercy on us according to your love.
           Wash away our wrongdoing and cleanse us from our sin.

31

> Renew a right spirit within us
> and restore us to the joy of your salvation,
> through Jesus Christ our Lord.
> **Amen.** *T&S All Saints to Advent*

President   Almighty God,
who in Jesus Christ has given us
a kingdom that cannot be destroyed,
forgive us our sins,
open our eyes to God's truth,
strengthen us to do God's will
and give us the joy of his kingdom,
through Jesus Christ our Lord.
Amen. *Main Volume p. 136*

Praise

Minister   Yours, Lord, is the greatness, the power,
the glory, the splendour and the majesty;
for everything in heaven and on earth is yours.

Yours, Lord, is the kingdom:
and you are exalted as head over all. Amen.
T&S All Saints to Advent

Praise songs

The Liturgy of the Word

Readings

Deuteronomy 6.1–9
Sung responsorial Psalm: 119.1–8
Hebrews 9.11–14
Sung alleluias
Mark 12.28–34   *CW Lectionary, 4 before Advent*

Sermon

Affirmation of Faith

Credal hymn: 'We believe in God the Father'
Main Volume p. 146

Prayers

Intercessions and thanksgivings

President We pray for the coming of God's kingdom.

Minister	You sent your Son to bring good news to the poor,
	sight to the blind,
	freedom to captives
	and salvation to your people:
	anoint us with your Spirit;
	rouse us to work in his name.
	Father, by your Spirit
	bring in your kingdom.

Send us to bring help to the poor
and freedom to the oppressed.
Father, by your Spirit
bring in your kingdom.

Send us to tell the world
the good news of your healing love.
Father, by your Spirit
bring in your kingdom.

Send us to those who mourn,
to bring joy and gladness instead of grief.
Father, by your Spirit
bring in your kingdom.

Send us to proclaim that the time is here
for you to save your people.
Father, by your Spirit
bring in your kingdom.

President	Lord of the Church,
All	**hear our prayer,**
	and make us one in mind and heart
	to serve you in Christ our Lord. Amen.

T&S All Saints to Advent

Collect

President	Almighty and eternal God,
	you have kindled the flame of love
	in the hearts of the saints:
	grant to us the same faith and power of love,

that, as we rejoice in their triumphs,
we may be sustained by their example and fellowship;
through Jesus Christ your Son our Lord,
who is alive and reigns with you,
in the unity of the Holy Spirit,
one God, now and for ever.

All   **Amen.**   *Main Volume, p. 423*

The Lord's Prayer

Conclusion

*Procession During the hymn 'For all the saints': at this point the
members of Junior Church joined the main congregation. They
all carried brightly coloured painted banners celebrating a great
variety of saints, and helium balloons. The Junior Church had
made the banners over the previous two weeks and that morning
had decorated them with tinsel, glitter and silver and gold stars.
The whole congregation, led by crucifer, acolytes and the children,
went in procession around the church, through the narthex and
into the church car park, which was situated on a busy main road.*

President Praise God for all his saints.

**All   Alleluia!
Like a cloud of witnesses they surround us.
Alleluia!
Like them, let us look to Jesus.
Alleluia!**

Minister Jesus said: All authority in heaven and on earth has
been given to me. Go, therefore and make disciples of
all the nations.   *T&S All Saints to Advent*

The balloons are released and everyone cheers.

President Christ our King make you faithful and strong to do his
will,
that you may reign with him in glory;
and the blessing of God almighty,
the Father, the Son, and the Holy Spirit,
be among you and remain with you always.

All   **Amen.**   *T&S All Saints to Advent*

Minister Go in the peace of Christ.

All **Thanks be to God.**

The whole service lasted 55 minutes. The role of the children and
the banners was crucial, as it brought parents and other members
of the family along. There were good quality refreshments, and
photographs were taken of the children and the banners. The
helium balloons had a greeting from All Saints' Church attached.
The vicar, and all who assisted, made every effort to ensure that
the service was accessible, vibrant and challenging.

In many ways, both the more traditional and 'highbrow' Sung
Eucharist and this Service of the Word were inspired by mission
imperatives; the former was beautiful, impressive, choral; the
latter more informal, inclusive and straightforward. Both have a
place in today's culture and within the life of the same church.

Thanksgiving for the Holy Ones of God

This litany, adapted in *Promise* from a Franciscan original, has
proved to be a popular form of thanksgiving for use during All
Saintstide. The text has been further revised, with suggested
congregational responses after each group of three commemorations.
It may be used at Morning and Evening Prayer, as a processional
(look out for musical settings and resources), or as part of a specially
constructed order of service.

Thanksgiving for the Holy Ones of God

The following responses may be said or sung

Let us bless the Lord.

Thanks be to God.

(or)

Alleluia, alleluia, alleluia.

For Abraham and Sarah, our ancestors in faith,
and all who journey into the unknown trusting God's promises:

For Jacob, deceitful younger brother, yet chosen by God,
the father of all who are called by virtue not of their own:

For Moses the lawgiver and Aaron the priest,
and all who lead God's people to freedom and newness of
    life: **R**

For Esther and Deborah, saviours of their nation,
and for all who dare to act courageously at God's call:

For Hannah and Ruth, and all who through love and devotion
witness to the faithfulness of God:

For Isaiah, John the Baptist and all the prophets,
and all who speak the truth without counting the cost: **R**

For Mary the Virgin, the mother of our Lord and God,
and all who obey God's call without question:

For Andrew and John and the first disciples,
and for all who forsake everything to follow Jesus:

For Mary Magdalene, Salome and Mary,
first witnesses of the resurrection,
and for all who bear witness to Christ: **R**

For Peter and Paul [, N] and the apostles,
who preached the gospel to Jew and Gentile,
and for all who take the good news to the ends of the earth:

For Barnabas, Silas and Timothy,
And for all who bring encouragement and steadfastness:

*In the following sections names may be added or omitted
to reflect local traditions.*

For the writers of the Gospels
and for all who bring the faith of Christ alive for each
    generation: **R**

For Ambrose, Augustine, Gregory and Jerome,
and for all who contend for the truth of the gospel:

For Basil, Gregory of Nazianzus, Athanasius and John
     Chrysostom,
and all who enable us to reflect on the mystery of Christ:

For Cyprian, Antony and Ephrem,
and for all who lead the Church into new paths of
     discipleship: *R*

For Stephen, Alban, Agnes, Lucy and the whole army of martyrs,
and all who have faced death for love of Christ:

For Augustine of Canterbury and Aidan, for Boniface and
     Patrick,
and for all who have carried the gospel to this and other lands:

For Aelred, Bernard and Cuthbert,
and for all who live and teach the love of God: *R*

For Anselm and Richard Hooker,
and for all who reveal to us the depths of God's wisdom:

For Benedict and Francis, Hilda and Bede,
and for all who deepen our common life in Christ:

For Julian of Norwich, Bridget of Sweden and Teresa of Avila,
and for all who renew our vision of the mystery of God: *R*

For Thomas Cranmer
and all who reform the Church of God:

For Thomas More
and all who hold firm to its continuing faith:

For Gregory and Dunstan, George Herbert and John Keble,
and for all who praise God in poetry and song: *R*

For Lancelot Andrewes, John Wesley, and Charles Simeon,
and for all who preach the word of God:

For William Wilberforce and Josephine Butler,
and for all who work to transform the world:

For Monica, and for Mary Sumner,
and for all who nurture faith in home and family: **R**

For the martyrs and peacemakers of our own time,
who shine as lights in the darkness:

For all the unsung heroes and heroines of our faith,
whose names are known to God alone:

For all those in our own lives
who have revealed to us the love of God
and shown to us the way of holiness: **R**

For (NN . . .) **R**

Let us rejoice and praise them with thankful hearts
and glorify our God in whom they put their trust.

The following may be used

The Lord's Prayer

The Collect of All Saints' Day

May the infinite and glorious Trinity,
the Father, the Son, and the Holy Spirit,
direct our life in good works,
and after our journey through this world,
grant us eternal rest with the saints.
Amen.

In using the text, the following possibilities should be noted:

- the text is divided into two by a rubric, allowing names to be added or omitted to reflect local traditions in the second half of the litany;

- where the patron saint of a church is an apostle other than Andrew, John, Peter and Paul, the appropriate name(s) may be inserted where indicated;

- the final petition is open for the use of any appropriate names.

A Service of Readings

The Promise of His Glory included resources in its 'The Service of Light' section for non-sacramental Services of Readings with three main elements:

- the Service of Light

- Patterns for Readings, with Psalms, Canticles, and Collects

- At the Conclusion: The Gospel Proclamation

This material was flexible: not all three elements had to be used, and the suggested forms could be freely adapted. In *Common Worship*, the Service of Light material is now found in *Common Worship: Daily Prayer* (pp. 110–11), but the principles and structures in *Promise* can still be used fruitfully.

One possibility would be to have an evening Service of Light and Readings for 31 October, Halloween, to restore it as a genuine vigil of All Saints rather than an occasion for the occultist or frivolous 'trick or treat' associations which seem ever to increase. The following order draws on and adapts *Promise* material.

Service for the Eve of All Saints' Day

The Service of Light
(see *CW: Daily Prayer* pp. 110–111)

The church is in darkness

Responsory or sentence

The bringing in or lighting of a candle or lamp

Greeting

Light Prayer (see *CW: Daily Prayer* p. 297)

'Phos hilaron', or some other hymn, *with lighting of congregational candles*

Psalm 141 *if desired. Incense may be burned.*

Introduction

> Dear friends, as we begin to celebrate the great festival of the saints in light, we gather in vigil to hear God's word and

to rejoice in the triumph of the saints through the saving power of Jesus Christ our Lord.

Let us therefore pray that God will banish the darkness of sin and evil and bring in his kingdom of justice and joy.

Silence is kept.

The Collect

The Liturgy of the Word

Readings and psalmody

Gospel Reading: the Gospel for All Saints' Day with preceding acclamation

Canticle: *Te Deum Laudamus or another suitable canticle, hymn or song*

Thanksgiving for the Holy Ones of God

Thanksgiving for the Holy Ones of God, or prayers of intercession may be used

The Lord's Prayer

The Dismissal

The congregation may go in procession to the font or to a suitable chapel or place in the church.

Dismissal Gospel

Blessing and dismissal

Patterns of readings

In the above service, various patterns of readings may be used, illustrating some of the themes of All Saintstide. While the suggestions below include six readings and a Gospel reading, selections may be made according to time and circumstance.

1 The Saints

1. Genesis 12.1–8
   Psalm 113
2. Daniel 6.(1–15) 16–23
   Psalm 116.1–9

3. Ecclesiasticus 44.1–10, 13–14 *or* Isaiah 56.3–8
   Psalm 148
4. Isaiah 43.1–7
   Psalm 91.9–16
5. Hebrews 11.32–12.1
   A Song of the Redeemed (Behold a great multitude)
6. Revelation 21.1–4, 22–22.5
   A Song of the Lamb (Salvation and glory and power)

2 Women Saints

1. Isaiah 61.1–3a
   A Song of the Bride (I will greatly rejoice in the Lord)
2. Proverbs 8.1–11 *or* Proverbs 31.10–end
   Psalm 119.1–8
3. Song of Solomon 4.8–12; 8.6–7
   Psalm 45.10–end
4. Ecclesiasticus 2.7–13
   Psalm 123
5. Romans 8.22–27 *or* Philippians 4.4–9
   Psalm 19.8–end
6. 1 John 2.15–17 or 2 Corinthians 10.17–11.2
   A Song of the Lamb (Salvation and glory and power)

3 Men Saints

1. 1 Kings 19.9–18 *or* Malachi 2.5–7
   Psalm 119.97–104
2. Micah 6.6–8
   Psalm 15
3. Isaiah 6.1–8
   Psalm 40.8–13
4. Ecclesiasticus 39.1–10 *or* 15.1–6
   Psalm 34.11–18
5. Wisdom 7.7–16 *or* Proverbs 4.2–9
   Psalm 119.89–96
6. 1 Corinthians 2.6–10, 13–16 *or* Philippians 3.7–14 *or* 2 Timothy 4.1–8
   A Song of God's Grace (Blessed are you, the God and Father of our Lord Jesus Christ)

4 Martyrs

1. 2 Esdras 2.42–end
   Psalm 126

2. Jeremiah 15.15–21
   Psalm 124
3. Ecclesiasticus 51.1–12
   Psalm 116.1–8
4. Wisdom 4.10–15 *or* Jeremiah 11.18–20
   Psalm 3
5. 2 Maccabees 6.18, 21, 24–31 *or* 2 Chronicles 24.16–21
   Psalm 31.1–8, 17–18
6. 1 Peter 4.12–end *or* James 1.12–18 *or* Hebrews 10.32–38a
   A Song of the Redeemed (Behold a great multitude)

5 Victory over the Powers of Darkness

1. 1 Samuel 28.3–19 *or* 1 Samuel 17.32–50
   Psalm 3
2. Job 2.1–10
   Psalm 13
3. Daniel 3.8–14, 16–26
   Psalm 124
4. Ephesians 6.10–18
   Psalm 27.1–6
5. Colossians 1.9–15
   Psalm 91. 1–8
6. Revelation 12.7–12
   A Song of the Holy City (I saw a new heaven and a new earth)
7. Gospel Reading (*this pattern of readings only*) John 17.6–19

Eve of All Saints with Children

Some churches may wish to hold an All Saints' Eve 'Light Party' or other event to counter the more negative aspects of Halloween. (Suggestions can be found in Nick Harding, *Better than Halloween*, Church House Publishing, 2006.) This may include games, preparation for all-age worship on All Saints' Sunday, and a short act of worship. For example, simple banners or posters may be made commemorating a variety of saints or other holy men or women, decorated with ribbons, brightly coloured paper and glitter. These may then be used in church as part of All Saintstide worship. With appropriate supervision, candles, lanterns, or sparklers may be used. Or children may dress up as 'saints' in simple costumes, or a frieze may be made. One or more of the following prayers may be used.

Lord Jesus Christ, Light of the world,
even though it is dark outside
you shine upon us to give us light and warmth.
Keep us in your love this night,
and bless our homes and families.
Amen.

Lord Jesus Christ, Light of the world,
your light has shone in the hearts of millions of people
throughout history.
Thank you for all the saints,
for all who have served you here on earth
and now are with you for ever in heaven.
Help us to love and serve you today.
Amen.

Lord Jesus Christ, Light of the world,
sometimes we are frightened, sometimes we are scared.
Thank you that you promise to be with us.
Thank you that we can know you as a friend.
Amen.

Lord Jesus Christ, Light of the world,
thank you for the family of the Church.
Thank you that here we think about all that is good
and true and lovely.
Help us to become more like you,
and to share the good things you give us.
Amen.

Celebrating Initiation in All Saintstide

Common Worship: Christian Initiation provides seasonal material
for the period from All Saints' Day to Advent. Here, the focus is on
incorporation into the people of God. The 'Celebration of Baptism
and Confirmation within a Vigil Service' reflects the propriety of All
Saintstide as a baptismal season, along with Epiphany, Easter and
Pentecost. Full seasonal material for the celebration of baptism in this
period is given on pp. 161–5 of *Common Worship: Christian Initiation*.

Rites on the Way

Rites on the Way provides material to support the initiation of those able to answer for themselves. It encourages people to explore the Christian faith as an accompanied journey, of no fixed duration, but leading to a staged process of initiation. So those who come to the point in their journey of faith when they desire fully and consciously to prepare for the rites of initiation undertake a public ceremony entitled the Call ('Call and Celebration of the Decision to be Baptized or Confirmed, or to Affirm Baptismal Faith'), and the final period of preparation may be marked by study and consideration of the 'Four Texts' (Jesus' Summary of the Law, The Lord's Prayer, The Apostles' Creed, The Beatitudes) which may be presented liturgically during Sunday Worship on four successive weeks. This then leads to the celebration of Initiation, and a later post-Initiation thanksgiving and commissioning. Page 332 of *Common Worship: Christian Initiation* sets out how this may be structured for initiation at All Saints:

Call	Holy Cross Day (14 September) or the nearest Sunday
Presentation of the Four Texts	The last four Sundays after Trinity
Baptism, Confirmation Affirmation, Reception	All Saints' Day or All Saints' Sunday
Thanksgiving and Sending Out	Christ the King, or later

All Souls' Day

The Commemoration of the Faithful Departed or All Souls' Day falls on 2 November, although many churches observe it on the Sunday nearest, possibly in the evening. It is a Lesser Festival in *Common Worship*, but is widely observed in churches of a more catholic tradition. Some Anglicans can find very little theological space between All Saints' Day and All Souls' and are distrustful of the historic links between the latter and the doctrine of purgatory in the Roman Catholic tradition, as well as theological unease around the question of prayer for the departed.

However, in recent years, a pastoral case for the observance of All Souls has been made, seeing it as complementary to the feast of All Saints. If All Saints is a triumphant and joyful celebration of the communion of all the saints in the mystical Body of Christ, All Souls is a more reflective and personal remembering of those whom 'we love but see no longer'. In this sense, it recognizes continuing bereavement and loss and gives opportunity, in the presence of God, for the expression of continuing bonds of love and affection. In some churches, the traditional liturgical colours of purple/violet or black will be used (although the latter could give entirely the wrong signals), or gold/white or red may be used (the latter especially if red is the adopted colour for the pre-Advent period).

The Eucharist of the Commemoration of the Faithful Departed

Times and Seasons follows *The Promise of His Glory* in providing a structure with the act of commemoration in the post-communion. The rite as far as the distribution of communion follows Order 1 with the following seasonal texts:

- an introduction to confession

- a Kyrie Confession as an alternative to the general confession 'Father eternal'

- Gospel acclamation

- a form of Intercession, adapted from the form in *Promise*

- introduction to the Peace

- short and extended Prefaces

- a form for the breaking of the bread from *Promise*

- words of invitation to communion from *Promise*

The Commemoration, coming immediately after the distribution of communion, also follows the *Promise* provision, slightly adapted.

The text of the commemoration runs:

Acclamation ('Glory and honour and power . . .')

The names of those to be remembered may be read aloud. Silence may be kept after each name, or group of names, or after all the names have been read.

Either **A**

This is the will of him that sent me,
that I should lose nothing of all that he has given me,
and I will raise them up at the last day.

Lord God, creator of all,
you have made us creatures of this earth,
but have also promised us a share in life eternal.
According to your promises,
may all who have died in the peace of Christ
come with your saints to the joy of your kingdom,
where there is neither sorrow nor pain,
but life everlasting.
Alleluia! Amen.

Grant to us, Lord God,
to trust you not for ourselves alone,
but for those also whom we love
and who are hidden from us by the shadow of death;
that, as we believe your power to have raised our Lord Jesus
    Christ from the dead,
so we may trust your love
to give eternal life to all who believe in him;
through Jesus Christ our Lord,
who is alive and reigns with you and the Holy Spirit,
one God, now and for ever.
Amen.

Or **B**

The Russian 'Kontakion for the departed', *followed by*

Hear us, O merciful Father,
as we remember in love

those whom we have placed in your hands.
Acknowledge, we pray, the sheep of your own fold,
lambs of your own flock,
sinners of your own redeeming.
Enfold them in the arms of your mercy,
in the blessed rest of everlasting peace,
and in the glorious company of the saints in light.
Amen.

The service concludes with the Prayer after Communion, blessing
(simple or extended) and dismissal, including the text:

Neither death nor life
can separate us from the love of God
in Jesus Christ our Lord.
Thanks be to God.

While this structure works well, experience of using it suggests that
the commemoration should not be excessive in terms of time or the
service may lose some of its pastoral effectiveness by being *too* long
or too over-loaded towards the end.

Alternative Structure

For this reason, some churches will prefer the more traditional pattern
for the commemoration as part of or replacing the Intercession. Where
commemoration is incorporated into the form of intercession this can
be done as follows:

Jesus, our way and truth and life,
you drew your disciple Thomas from doubt to faith:
reveal the resurrection faith to the doubting and the lost.

Hear us, risen Lord,
our resurrection and our life.

Jesus our hope, we remember in your presence those whom
we love and see no longer.

Here names may be read, and/or silence kept.

> Hear us, risen Lord,
> **our resurrection and our life.**
>
> May God in his infinite love and mercy . . .

Alternatively, material from the Commemoration may be used here, following or replacing the prayers. The service then continues with the Peace.

Non-Eucharistic services

There is a strong and growing tradition of inviting recent mourners to an All Soulstide service or, in parishes with many funerals, to periodic memorial services. While in some churches such services will be eucharistic, others judge that a simple non-eucharistic rite is more pastorally helpful. *Times and Seasons* does not provide a non-eucharistic order, although the material in the Eucharist is easily adaptable to a Word service. However, a sample form of memorial service is given in *Common Worship: Pastoral Services* (pp. 331–44), with a comprehensive bank of resource material (pp. 345–401). While few, if any, would wish to make such a service overtly evangelistic, many churches have discovered that the opportunity to show care for the bereaved and to set their loss in the context of Christian hope through liturgy, sermon, and music, opens up for some the possibility of finding or re-finding faith and an ongoing relationship with the local Christian community.

How to remember

In many churches, there is a long-established tradition of reading names of loved ones at All Soulstide. This has much to commend it, as names are personal and honoured. It can present a difficulty, however, when there are very many names to read out, as well as the obvious practical task of ensuring fail-safe administration! There are other possibilities:

- presenting a book of remembrance at the altar or holy table in silence or while reflective music is played;
- inviting members of the congregation to light candles in memory of loved ones;
- inviting members of the congregation to place a flower or card at a place of remembrance in the church building;

- having names incorporated in the order of service, but not reading them, and inviting the lighting of candles in silence or while suitable music is played.

At St Michael's, there was a long-standing tradition of an evening Communion on All Souls' Day, with the reading of names at the Commemoration, using the *Times and Seasons* material. However, this service attracted only church members and normally about 40 names were submitted.

The parish was residential and the church had about 100 funerals a year. As the crematorium was local, the majority of funerals were held there and the clergy and licensed Reader were often frustrated by the constraints on time. The church decided to hold a memorial service twice a year on a Sunday evening in March and November, to which bereaved families were personally invited. At the front of the church, a large cross was placed to the left of the nave altar and the paschal candle to the right of it. Votive candle stands were placed before the cross and candle. Using material for memorial services in *Pastoral Services* and prayers from the All Souls' provision in *Times and Seasons*, the rector devised a simple service of prayers and readings, including a carefully prepared seven-minute sermon. As streams of people arrived, stewards wrote the names of those to be remembered on attractively produced cards; the cards were given to the bereaved families. At the commemoration, the rector led a short prayer of thanksgiving for those who had died, then, as the choir sang an anthem, members of the congregation were invited to lay the cards before the altar and light a candle at the candle stands; stewards were on hand to assist them with tapers. The atmosphere was very still, very focused. People seemed to appreciate the opportunity to *do* something, and it took about ten minutes for everyone to light the candles, creating a still centre in the service. After the commemoration the church lights were dimmed, leaving the cross and paschal candle illuminated by the tea-lights. The choir sang the anthem, 'God be in my head', the rector said the blessing and the lights were raised. Everyone seemed to be very appreciative and valued the invitation to come to church after the trauma of bereavement and the very short and stark rite of passage afforded by the Crem.

The Sunday following the November service was Remembrance Sunday, when the wreaths were also laid before the cross and paschal candle; as the church was open for part of each day, further names had been added and the church became a focus of corporate remembrance for that community.

Christ Church is an evangelical church. It does not observe All Souls' Day, but it does take its ministry to the bereaved very seriously. Funeral ministry is exercised with great care, and a lay team of bereavement visitors are conscientious in their pastoral follow-up.

The church hosts two memorial services each year, which the recently bereaved are invited to attend. The church is happy to commemorate the departed and pray for the bereaved, but there is no tradition of praying for the dead as such, especially if that suggests that such prayer might influence their salvation.

The church music group forms itself into a small choir for these occasions. The names of all whose funerals have been conducted by the parish since the last Memorial Service are printed in the front cover of the attractively produced service booklet. At the commemoration, three ministers, two ordained and one lay, read in turn the names of the departed, each minister reading four names at a time. The names are read slowly and there is good use of silence. The memorial service draws on some material in the All Souls section of *Times and Seasons* and some from the memorial section of *Common Worship: Pastoral Services* and has the following structure.

The Gathering

Welcome

Hymn   'Praise to the Lord, the Almighty'

Greeting

Sentence of Scripture: Matthew 11.28, 29

Preface   We have come together in our Father's presence
               to remember our loved ones

who have passed through the valley of the shadow of
    death;
to renew our faith and trust in God;
to pray for those who mourn;
and to seek God's grace,
that we may know his love, and the hope he gives us,
through faith in Jesus Christ.
Let us therefore remember God's presence with us now.

Prayers of penitence (from the All Souls' Service)

Collect

Liturgy of the Word

First Lesson

Psalm 121 (said responsively)

Second Lesson

Hymn   'The King of love my shepherd is'

Sermon

Choir Anthem   'The Lord bless you and keep you' John Rutter

Apostles' Creed

Prayers

Prayers of intercession include prayer for the bereaved, led by the
lay bereavement visitors

The Lord's Prayer

Hymn

The Commemoration
A time of silent prayer is kept.

Minister Be still and know that I am God.

        The eternal God is your refuge,
        and underneath are the everlasting arms.

        Blessed are those who mourn,
        for they shall be comforted.

        God of compassion and love,
        we remember before you with thanksgiving

> those whom we love but see no longer.
> *Here the names to be remembered are read aloud*
>
> Grant us, Lord God,
> to trust you not for ourselves alone,
> but for those we love
> who are hidden from us by the shadow of death;
> that, as we believe your power to have raised
>   Jesus Christ from the dead,
> so may we trust you
> to give eternal life to all who believe in him;
> through Jesus Christ our Lord,
> who is alive and reigns with you and the Holy Spirit,
> one God, now and for ever. **Amen.**

Choir Anthem   'A Clare Blessing'   John Rutter

Hymn   'I will sing the wondrous story'

The Blessing

After the service, good quality refreshments were served in the church hall. The service and the pastoral contact it enabled was an important part of the church's call to serve its parish and build up good relationships within the community.

Remembrance Sunday

In *The Promise of His Glory*, the 1968 ecumenical Remembrance Day service was reproduced in its entirety. This service has now been superseded by a new 2005 order, commended by the presidents of Churches Together in Britain and Ireland. The service was compiled by an ecumenical group convened by CTBI in conjunction with the Royal British Legion, as guardians of the nation's remembrance, and the (ecumenical) Joint Liturgical Group. The order is centred on an act of remembrance, which may be out of doors and can be supplemented by additional resources. The material is easily adaptable for incorporation into a Eucharist or Service of the Word. *Times and Seasons* also includes the introduction to remembrance from the 1968 order and a form of words introducing the Peace (see pp. 582–5).

The CTBI service, as well as remembering the fallen of two World Wars and other conflicts since, takes full account of civilian loss, the reality of terrorism and the longing for peace and security throughout the world. Notes in the text deal with the practicalities to be thought through. The structure of the rite is:

Gathering

Sentence(s) from the Hebrew Scriptures

Introduction: We meet in the presence of God.

We commit ourselves to work
in penitence and faith
for reconciliation between the nations,
that all people may, together,
live in freedom, justice and peace.

We pray for all
who in bereavement, disability and pain
continue to suffer the consequences of fighting
    and terror.

We remember with thanksgiving and sorrow
those whose lives,
in world wars and conflicts past and present,
have been given and taken away.

Remembering

Binyon's words 'They shall grow not old . . .'

Two minutes' silence

Prayer

Hymn ('O God our help', or other)

Listening for the word from God

Reading from the New Testament

Praying Together

Intercession

The Lord's Prayer

Responding in Hope and Commitment

The Kohima Epitaph ('When you go home . . .')

(Hymn)

Act of Commitment	Let us commit ourselves to responsible living and faithful service.
	Will you strive for all that makes for peace? **We will.**
	Will you seek to heal the wounds of war? **We will.**
	Will you work for a just future for all humanity? **We will.**
	Merciful God, we offer to you the fears in us that have not yet been cast out by love: may we accept the hope you have placed in the hearts of all people, and live lives of justice, courage and mercy; through Jesus Christ our risen redeemer. **Amen.**
National Anthem(s)	
Blessing	

Other resources may be found in the CTBI volume *Beyond our Tears: Resources for Times of Remembrance* and in the 1994 *Book of Common Order* of the Church of Scotland (pp. 409–20).

Christ the King

The Feast of Christ the King is a festival in *Common Worship*, falling on the last Sunday of the liturgical year. Introduced into the Roman calendar for the last Sunday in October by Pope Pius XI in 1925, it was moved to the end of the liturgical year in 1970, and adopted by the Church of England in 2000. It has been criticized as a duplication of Ascension Day or as implying by its new position at the end of the Christian Year that Christ is not yet reigning. However, part of Pius XI's original intention was to affirm the Lordship of Christ over all political and social systems, given the rise of fascism and communism in the early twentieth century, and this political dimension gives Christ the King a rather different context to that of the Ascension. Moreover, the eschatological context of this pre-Advent period reminds us that the kingship of Christ involves judgement, lest mercy be emptied of any real meaning.

The Invitation to Confession, first Gospel Acclamation, Extended Preface, and second short Blessing are from the All Saints to Advent seasonal provision in the *Main Volume*, and the extended Blessing from the *President's Edition*. However, there are some new texts:

Kyrie Confession Adapted from the doxology to the Lord's Prayer.

The kingdom is yours,
but we turn away from your just rule:
Lord, have mercy.
Lord, have mercy.

The power is yours,
but we trust in our own power and strength:
Christ, have mercy.
Christ, have mercy.

The glory is yours,
but we fall short of the glory of God:
Lord, have mercy.
Lord, have mercy.

Gospel Acclamation An alternative is provided, based on the Te Deum: 'You Christ are the King of glory, the eternal Son of the Father'.

Intercession A form for Christ the King from Gail Ramshaw (ed.), *Intercessions for the Christian People* (Pueblo Publishing Company, 1988).

Introduction to the Peace From *New Patterns*, based on Colossians 3.14, 15.

Prayer at the Preparation of the Table A new prayer alluding to
Ephesians 2.6 and to Horatius Bonar's hymn 'Here, O my Lord':

> Blessed be God,
> who enthrones us with Christ in the heavenly realms.
> May we feed upon the bread of God
> and drink the royal wine of heaven.
> **Blessed be God for ever.**

Prefaces The first relates to Christ's self-offering:

> And now we give you thanks
> because you anointed Jesus Christ, your only Son,
> as priest and King.
> Crowned with thorns, he offered his life upon the cross,
> that he might draw all people into that kingdom
> where now he reigns in glory.

The second is a summary of the Extended Preface.

Short Passages of Scripture Five texts are provided. The first, from Mark
11, could be used as a versicle and response:

> Blessed is the one who comes in the name of the Lord.
> **Blessed is the coming kingdom of our ancestor David.**

The following three texts are all suitable for the Gathering or at the
Preparation of the Table; the final text, the 'great commission' from
Matthew 28 is suitable for the Dismissal.

3 Advent

> Pour down, O heavens, from above,
> and let the skies rain down righteousness.
> Let the earth be fruitful and bring forth a Saviour.
> *Advent Prose*

People, look east

As the introduction to Advent in *Times and Seasons* states, Advent is
a time of expectation and preparation. The season embraces both a
period of preparation for the coming of Christmas and the call to be
ready for the final in-breaking of the kingdom in power as Christ
comes again in glory as judge and king. We can tease out a number
of distinctive moods and themes.

Joyful expectation Both in the sense that, at last, the promises to Israel
are about to be fulfilled in the coming of the Son of God into the
world, and in anticipating the great hope of the return of Christ to
usher in the life of the world to come and complete the new creation.

Hope Because in the darkness of sin a new light has dawned in Christ,
who is faithful to his promises to inaugurate a new heaven and new
earth in which righteousness dwells.

Recollection The coming of Christ was to lead us to repentance and
into an experience of forgiveness through his incarnation, saving death
and passion, and glorious resurrection, and he will come again as judge
of the living and the dead.

Discipleship The call to holiness, as we pray that when he comes the
Lord may find in us a mansion prepared for himself.

Three comings

In Christian spirituality, Advent has embraced the great mystery of the
coming of the Word made flesh at Christmas, the final coming or
parousia of the Son of Man in glory at the consummation of all things,

and the great truth that Christ *comes* in word, in sacrament, in the hearts and lives of Christians and by the power of his Spirit. The great Aramaic cry of the earliest Christian communities, *Marana tha* – Come, Lord (Jesus), is as much a cry for today as for the future.

A mixed economy

These themes overlap in Scripture, hymnody, song, symbol and prayer. So for example, anticipation and penitence mingle in the great hymn, 'Hark, a thrilling voice':

> Hark, a thrilling voice is sounding;
> 'Christ is nigh,' it seems to say;
> 'Cast away the dreams of darkness,
> O ye children of the day.'
>
> Lo, the Lamb, so long expected,
> comes with pardon down from heaven;
> let us haste, with tears of sorrow,
> one and all to be forgiven.
>
> *Sixth century*

Purple (or blue), traditionally the penitential liturgical colour, is used for the season; however, this is not a mini Lent, and the use of purple indicates more the sense that God's ultimate promises are awaiting fulfilment. Traditionally, *Gloria in excelsis* is not used at the Eucharist; as it echoes the message of the angels to the shepherds, it is held back until Christmas. However, unlike Lent, the gospel Alleluias are retained, and there is a strong note of joy and gladness:

> Hark, the glad sound! The Saviour comes,
> the Saviour promised long:
> let every heart prepare a throne,
> and every voice a song.
>
> *Philip Doddridge*

Indeed, Advent comes at the *end* of the calendar year, but it *begins* the Christian year; it celebrates the *genesis* of the story of salvation through Christ while pointing us to the *consummation* of all things in Christ. It is the season of the darkest of days, but, anticipating Christmas, embraces the winter solstice, heralding the rise of the 'Sun of Righteousness' (Malachi 4.2).

Common Worship invites us to consider the season in two halves. The first half is from Advent Sunday to December 16, when traditionally the church has reflected on the 'four last things': death, judgement, heaven and hell. Here again, Christian hope and the darker themes of mortality and judgement mingle, and call us to penitence and humility before the consuming holiness of God as we seek his mercy. In the second half, from December 17, the emphasis changes to direct preparation for the great festival of Christmas, in order that Christ may be born in us, with hearts and minds renewed.

Finding a route through

This mixture of pieties can cause confusion. The *Common Worship* Principal Service Lectionary, however, seeks to provide a rationale. The controlling Gospel reading focuses on the Second Coming (Advent 1), John the Baptist (Advent 2 and 3) and the Annunciation stories (Advent 4).

Advent 1

Eschatological themes dominate; this is the completion of the eschatological themes which run through the Sundays before Advent, focusing especially on the Second Coming (parousia).

Year A

Isaiah 2.1–5	He shall judge between nations
Psalm 122	Now our feet are standing within your gates, O Jerusalem
Romans 13.11–14	Now is the moment for you to wake out of sleep, our salvation is nearer
Matthew 24.36–44	The coming of the Son of Man.

Year B

Isaiah 64.1–9	O that you would tear open the heavens and come down
Psalm 80.1–8, 18–20	Stir up your mighty strength and come to our salvation
1 Corinthians 1.3–9	As you wait for the revealing of our Lord Jesus Christ
Mark 13.24–37	The Son of Man coming in clouds.

Year C

Jeremiah 33.14–16	I will cause a righteous Branch to spring up for David

Psalm 25.1–9	You are the God of my salvation
1 Thessalonians 3.9–13	You may be blameless at the coming of our Lord Jesus with all his saints
Luke 21.25–36	They will see the Son of Man coming with a cloud.

Advent 2

The first of two Sundays focusing on the beginning of the ministry of John the Baptist: 'Prepare the way of the Lord' is the dominant theme, which relates to our preparedness for the parousia as well as recalling the historical ministry of John and the longing for the appearance of the Messiah.

Year A

Isaiah 11.1–10	A shoot shall come out from the stock of Jesse
Psalm 72.1–7 (18–19)	May he come down like rain upon the mown grass
Romans 15.4–13	By the encouragement of the scriptures we might have hope
Matthew 3.1–12	Prepare the way of the Lord.

Year B

Isaiah 40.1–11	Comfort my people
Psalm 85.(1–2), 8–13	Mercy and truth are met together
2 Peter 3.8–15a	The day of the Lord will come like a thief
Mark 1.1–8	Prepare the way of the Lord.

Year C

Baruch 5.1–9 *or*	Arise, Jerusalem, look towards the east
Malachi 3.1–4	I am sending my messenger to prepare the way
Benedictus	
Philippians 1.3–11	The one who began the good work will bring it to completion by the day of Christ Jesus
Luke 3.1–6	Prepare the way of the Lord.

Advent 3

The second Sunday where the focus is on the Baptist, but here themes of justice, judgement and the in-breaking of the kingdom are strong.

Year A

Isaiah 35.1–10	Here is your God
Psalm 146.4–10	The Lord gives justice to those who suffer wrong
or Magnificat	
James 5.7–10	Be patient until the coming of the Lord
Matthew 11.2–11	Are you the one who is to come?

Year B

Isaiah 61.1–4, 8–11	The spirit of the Lord God is upon me
Psalm 126 *or* Magnificat	Restore again our fortunes, O God
1 Thessalonians 5.16–24	May you be kept sound and blameless at the coming of our Lord Jesus Christ
John 1.6–8, 19–28	He came as a witness, to testify to the light.

Year C

Zephaniah 3.14–20	The Lord, your God, is in your midst
Canticle: Isaiah 12.2–6	Great in your midst is the Holy One of Israel
Philippians 4.4–7	Rejoice – The Lord is near
Luke 3.7–18	The axe is lying at the root of the trees.

Advent 4

Here the focus is on the annunciation, to Joseph in the Matthean tradition, and to Mary in the Lukan tradition.

Year A

Isaiah 7.10–16	Look, the young woman is with child
Psalm 80.1–8 (18–20)	Stir up your mighty strength, and come
Romans 1.1–7	The gospel concerning his Son, who was descended from David according to the flesh
Matthew 1.18–25	She will bear a son, and you are to name him Jesus.

Year B

2 Samuel 7.1–11, 16	Your throne shall be established for ever
Magnificat	
or Psalm 89.1–4, 19–26	Your seed will I establish for ever

Romans 16.25–27	The revelation of the mystery that was kept secret for long ages
Luke 1.26–38	Here I am, the servant of the Lord.

Year C

Micah 5.2–5a	From you, Bethlehem, shall come a ruler
Magnificat	
or Psalm 80.1–8	Show the light of your countenance and we shall be saved
Hebrews 10.5–10	A body you have prepared for me
Luke 1.39–45 (46–55)	Blessed is she who believed that there would be a fulfilment

This gives shape to the principal celebrations in the parish, and while the Advent 2 and Advent 3 lections mingle anticipation of the first and second comings of Christ, Christian discipleship is in reality worked out in the 'the years of our Lord', the redeemed time between his first and second comings. The above scheme helps us to plan how we might explore the great Advent themes in a balanced way, supported by hymn and song and the rich liturgical resources provided by *Times and Seasons*.

Seasonal material

As with all sections of *Times and Seasons*, the bank of resources provides material for the Eucharist and a Service of the Word. On Sundays, the lectionary provision given above indicates what choices are appropriate. For Advent 4, specially written texts (sometimes called 'propers') for the Blessed Virgin Mary and Joseph from *Common Worship: Festivals* may appropriately be used.

Invitations to Confession The first text is suitable throughout the season; the second is particularly appropriate for Advent 2, and the third for Advent 3.

Kyrie Confessions Three forms are provided: the first is based on Psalm 85; the second is on the theme of judgement and complements the lections on the Baptist; the third is a devotion on the Christ who came, who comes and who will come.

Gospel Acclamation From the *Main Volume*, from Isaiah 40.3.

Intercessions Two forms are provided, the first a plea for Christ to come, employing the versicle and response:

> Maranatha:
> **Amen. Come, Lord Jesus.**

The second is a prayer from *Common Worship: Daily Prayer* for the coming of the kingdom and for active discipleship.

Introductions to the Peace Four texts are given, drawing on biblical imagery: the first from the *Main Volume* and the others from *New Patterns for Worship*.

Prayers at the Preparation of the Table Three forms are given: the first combines imagery from the early Christian document *The Didache*, with a quotation from Proverbs 9. 1, 2:

> As this bread was scattered
> and then gathered and made one,
> so may your Church be gathered into your kingdom.
> **Glory to you, O God, for ever.**
>
> Wisdom has built her a house;
> she has mixed her wine; she has set her table.
> **Glory to you, O God, for ever.**

The second and third are from the *Main Volume*: 'Look upon us in mercy not in judgement . . .', and a fuller rendering of the *Didache* text: 'As the grain once scattered . . .'

Prefaces Five short prefaces are given: the first, second and fifth are suitable throughout the season, the third relates to Advent 2 and 3, and the fourth to Advent 4. The Extended Prefaces are from the *Main Volume*.

Blessings and Endings Two 'simple' blessings and two extended or 'solemn' blessings are provided. The extended blessings are best reserved for principal celebrations. The endings are not dismissal texts, but could be used as part of a Word service or carol service.

Alternative Dismissal for Advent Sunday This text, with the repeated refrain 'come, Lord Jesus', is particularly suited to the eschatological focus of Advent Sunday, at the Eucharist, a Service of the Word, or a specially devised service.

The Dismissal Gospel This gives a sequence of Gospel reading, blessing and dismissal for an extended post-communion rite. The Gospel could be read effectively from the Advent Wreath.

Short Passages of Scripture Eight texts are provided, and suitable choices could be used as an introit, before or after the Bible reading, at the preparation of the table, as a post-communion sentence, or as a refrain running throughout an order of service.

Advent carol services

Like *The Promise of His Glory, Times and Seasons* does not provide fully worked out Advent carol services. Instead, it has drawn on the *Promise* resources, many of which have proved to be durable. The main point is that Advent carol services should be genuinely about Advent, and not simply early Christmas services. The themes of the kingdom, judgement, penitence, justice and preparation come out clearly in the three specimen Bidding Prayers and Introductions, while the four sequences of readings provide models for exploring the Scriptures. Churches are not limited to these; for example, the pattern of readings at Durham Cathedral mingles comfort and challenge.

1	Amos 5.18–21, 23–24	The prophet denounces the easy expectations of those whose religion is only outward show
2	Micah 6.6–8	The prophet proclaims what the Lord requires of his people
3	Isaiah 40.1–11	The prophet proclaims God's mercy and announces his coming as king and shepherd
4	Isaiah 35.1–10	The prophet foretells the coming of God's kingdom with blessings of healing, harmony and joy

| 5 Matthew 25.31–45 | Jesus tells a parable of the Last Judgement |
| 6 Revelation 21.22–24; 22.1–5 | The Christian prophet pictures the light and glory of the new Jerusalem |

Six forms of responsory are provided in *Times and Seasons*. The final two are concluding responsories; the others may be used as an introit or a response to a reading, or incorporated into the prayers.

Many services will wish to use 'darkness to light' imagery, and many churches have developed creative processional services with movement from the west (darkness) to the east (light). But that is only one way of using the material. For most people, it is the mixture of challenge and hope, and the resonance of the great Advent hymns, that speak so powerfully in a culture seeking hope through often painful realism.

The following is only one of a number of possible structures:

• Responsory; such as the Advent Prose

• Lighting of the Advent Wreath with prayer for the blessing of the light

• Greeting, Bidding Prayer and Lord's Prayer

• Sequence of readings and music

• Responsory, such as 'Restore, us, O Lord God of hosts . . .' (p. 48)

• Collect for Advent Sunday

• Blessing and ending, such as 'The night is far spent, the day is at hand' etc. (p. 49)

The Advent Wreath

The popularity of the Advent Wreath today doubtless owes much to generations of children devoted to *Blue Peter*! While there are many variations (and few churches would choose to use coat hangers and tinsel), the wreath is essentially a circular base decorated with evergreens, holding four coloured candles (normally red, purple or blue) and sometimes a central white 'Christ-candle' or 'King'. The four candles are lit, one for each of the four Sundays of Advent, and the central candle on Christmas Day.

Origins

While some trace the origin of the wreath to the commemoration on 13 December of the fourth-century martyr St Lucy (Lucia, 'light'), with the tradition, strong in Scandanavia, of the crowning of a young girl with a wreath incorporating four lit candles, the revival of this symbol in modern times probably originated in Germany. The Advent Wreath was popularized by a German Lutheran pastor called Heinrich Wichern (1808–81). He ministered in Hamburg and founded an orphanage, the Rauhe Haus. He recorded in his diary:

> At daily prayers around the organ there were twenty-three coloured candles. Every day an additional candle was lit by brother Hansen, with each new word of promise, and in the end all twenty-three candles shone like a crown of light to the praise of God.

The 'word of promise' refers to biblical texts, usually verses from the Old Testament foretelling the coming of the Messiah, read by one of the staff. While the text was read, a child would then light an additional candle each day.

Originally, the candles were simply placed near the organ and moved to beside the crib and Christmas tree on Christmas Eve. However, an architect friend of Wichern made a circular candle-stand, and so the idea of a wreath developed, decorated with evergreen fir as a symbol of eternal life.

Because many people visited the orphanage, the idea spread, for use both in the home and in church, but as few churches had daily acts of worship, the tradition of using four candles for each of the four Sundays in Advent developed. The fifth candle, to symbolize the birth of the Christ-child, was a later development.

A bold symbol?

The Advent Wreath can still be seen in the Rauhe Haus – it is six feet wide! Sadly, many churches use candle-stands that are made essentially for domestic settings. If the wreath is to be the central and dominant symbol in Advent, it needs to be sufficiently large to make a dramatic statement of the coming of the light of Christ. It should be positioned prominently in the church building to form a focus for Advent worship throughout the season.

Many churches use four coloured candles for the four Sundays in Advent, usually purple or blue (depending on which liturgical colour is used) or red. A central white or gold candle (sometimes called 'the King') is reserved for Christmas Day. Some churches use a pink candle for Advent 3, reflecting the medieval title Gaudete ('rejoice') Sunday, derived from the medieval introit and based on Philippians 4.4–5, 'Rejoice, the Lord is near' (see Year C, above), when rose-coloured eucharistic vestments were also worn. Some churches have restored this custom. Fir branches made a useful symbolic link with the Christmas tree, although any evergreens are suitable for decoration. Where churches hold daily services (Eucharist or offices) the Rauhe Haus tradition of lighting a daily candle in Advent can be followed by arranging tealights around the wreath or designing a wreath that provides for up to twenty-eight candles (the maximum number of days in Advent).

There is a growing tradition of replacing the coloured candles with white candles for the first Eucharist of Christmas, and retaining the wreath throughout the twelve days of Christmas or until the feast of Candlemas.

The wreath can also help us with the widespread tradition of not having flowers in Advent. Again, this should not be thought of as imitating Lent; rather, evergreens can come into their own as a symbol of life and hope.

All this means that there is a good case for making the wreath the primary Advent symbol. However, it also means that churches should use their resources and imaginations to ensure that the wreath is large enough to carry the symbolism.

The Advent Wreath in *Times and Seasons*

Two sets of texts are provided. The first set provides a choice of three prayers for each Sunday. The first two prayers are from *The Promise of His Glory* and follow the traditional scheme:

Advent 1	The Patriarchs
Advent 2	The Prophets
Advent 3	John the Baptist
Advent 4	The Virgin Mary
Christmas Day	The Christ

These prayers are particularly suitable when churches use a 'Jesse Tree' as part of their preparation for Christmas. As well as lighting a candle, the relevant symbols can be placed on the Jesse Tree, which may be positioned in proximity to the wreath. *Times and Seasons* does not provide resources for the use of the Jesse Tree; however, such resources are readily available.

The third prayer in each set is different. These are new texts drawing on traditional Advent imagery and employing the creative use of exhortation with the verbs 'awake', 'be glad', 'return', 'prepare' for the four Sundays. So for Advent 1:

People of God: awake!
The day is coming soon
when you shall see God face to face.
Remember the ways and the works of God.
God calls you out of darkness
to walk in the light of his coming.
You are God's children.
Lord, make us one as we walk with Christ
today and for ever.
Amen.

The text for Advent 4 looks towards the coming of Christmas:

People of God: prepare!
God, above all, maker of all,
is one with us in Christ.
Maranatha!
Come, Lord Jesus!

God, the mighty God,
bends down in love to earth.

Maranatha!
Come, Lord Jesus!

God with us; God beside us,
comes soon to the world he has made.
Maranatha!
Come, Lord Jesus!

We are God's children,
we seek the coming Christ.
Maranatha!
Come, Lord Jesus!

These wreath prayers can be used at a variety of places: at the beginning of worship, after the Gospel reading at the Eucharist or a reading at a Service of the Word, before the Peace, or after communion. A lot will depend on local circumstances; for example, if children and young people meet separately for part of the Sunday morning programme, most churches would wish to light the candles at the part of the service in which they are present.

Each position has its own rationale: lighting the wreath during the Gathering is a reminder that we meet together in the light of Christ; at a Bible reading it resonates with the truth that light breaks forth from God's word; at the Peace it reminds us that we are to walk together in the light and peace of Christ.

Using the Advent Wreath in the post-communion accords well with a development that is central to *Times and Seasons*. This is to strengthen the understanding that the church is sent out for mission, to live and speak the gospel. This is particularly effective in larger buildings, or where space has been created in a church building, when the congregation can gather around the wreath and then be sent out from it. So at the Eucharist the following pattern could be used:

- after communion, the congregation gathers at the wreath (perhaps while a hymn is sung);

- the candle is lit and the prayer said as a post-communion;

- a dismissal Gospel may be read or acclamations used;

- the blessing and dismissal conclude the service.

On Advent 2, for example, these texts could be used:

Processional Hymn: 'Hills of the North' (during which the congregation gathers at the wreath)

President   God our Father,
you spoke to the prophets of old
of a Saviour who would bring peace.
You helped them to spread the joyful message
of his coming kingdom.
Help us, as we prepare to celebrate his birth,
to share with those around us
the good news of your power and love.
We ask this through Jesus Christ,
the light who is coming into the world.

T & S p. 52

Minister   With love and compassion:
All   **Come, Lord Jesus!**

With judgement and mercy:
Come, Lord Jesus!

In power and glory:
Come, Lord Jesus!

In wisdom and truth:
Come, Lord Jesus!

Minister   Hear the Gospel of our Lord Jesus Christ according to Mark.
All   **Glory to you, O Lord.**

Jesus came to Galilee, proclaiming the good news of God, and saying, 'The time is fulfilled, and the kingdom of God has come near; repent and believe in the good news'.

This is the Gospel of the Lord.
All   **Praise to you, O Christ.**

President   May God himself, the God of peace,
make you perfect and holy,
and keep you safe and blameless, in spirit, soul and
body,

> for the coming of our Lord Jesus Christ;
> and the blessing of God almighty,
> the Father, the Son and the Holy Spirit,
> be among you and remain with you this day and
>   always.
>
> *All*   **Amen.**
>
> *Minister*   As we await our coming Saviour,
>   go in the peace of Christ.
> *All*   **Thanks be to God.**

The second set of texts provides for the wreath being lit at the Prayers of Penitence. This accords well with scriptural texts such as

> When the Lord comes, he will bring to light things now hidden in darkness and will disclose the purposes of the heart.
>
> *(I Corinthians 4.5)*

So the texts in this set for the third week of Advent are:

> Heavenly Father,
> you call us to prepare for the coming of your Son:
> forgive our unreadiness to receive him.
> Lord, have mercy.
> **Lord, have mercy.**
>
> Lord Jesus,
> you were proclaimed by John the Baptist:
> help us also to prepare your way.
> Christ, have mercy.
> **Christ, have mercy.**
>
> Holy Spirit,
> you speak through the prophets:
> make us attentive to hear your word.
> Lord, have mercy.
> **Lord, have mercy.**

This is particularly effective when the President invites the congregation to confession, silence is kept while the candles are lit, and the Kyrie Confession then follows.

Church and home

The Advent Wreath is a very good way of linking church and domestic celebrations. At home, candles may be lit every day or each Sunday, using any of the relevant *Times and Seasons* material. See also *Together for a Season: All-age seasonal resources for Advent, Christmas and Epiphany* (Church House Publishing, 2006).

Advent Antiphons

Historically, the Advent Antiphons were used before and after the Magnificat at Evening Prayer on the seven days preceding Christmas Eve. This use has been restored in *Common Worship: Daily Prayer* (p. 211). They are, of course, best known from the hymn 'O come, O come, Emmanuel', in the translations of J. M. Neale or T. A. Lacey. The antiphons all begin with 'O' and employ biblical names and titles, addressed to Christ as Messiah and Saviour:

17 December	O Wisdom	(O Sapientia)
18 December	O Adonai	(O Adonai)
19 December	O Root of Jesse	(O Radix Jesse)
20 December	O Key of David	(O Clavis David)
21 December	O Morning Star	(O Oriens)
22 December	O King of the Nations	(O Rex Gentium)
23 December	O Emmanuel	(O Emmanuel)

Times and Seasons includes special lectionary readings for Evening Prayer when the antiphons are used in their traditional setting (p. 52).

The antiphons and lectionary readings can be very easily adapted as a vigil service or Advent carol service. In *The Promise of His Glory*, a service built around the antiphons was included, with the structure:

The Entrance

- The Advent Prose
- Greeting
- Collect

The Ministry of the Word

A seven-fold sequence for each antiphon;

- Antiphon

- Response: **Amen. Come, Lord Jesus**

- Short reading   O Wisdom: Ecclesiasticus 24.3–9
                 O Adonai: Exodus 3.1–6
                 O Root of Jesse: Isaiah 11.1–4a
                 O Key of David: Isaiah 22.21–23
                 O Morning star: Numbers 24.15b–17
                 O King of the Nations: Jeremiah 30.7–11a
                 O Emmanuel: Matthew 1.18–23

- Corresponding verse of 'O come, O come, Immanuel'

The Celebration of Penitence and Reconciliation

- Examination of conscience

- Prayer for God's mercy

- Act of penitence and contrition

- Act of Absolution

- Lord's Prayer

The Conclusion

- Prayer of thanksgiving

- Blessing

- Dismissal

For 'The Celebration of Penitence and Reconciliation', new material from the Reconciliation and Restoration section of *Common Worship: Christian Initiation* can easily be adapted (see pp. 227–89).

The Advent Prose

This responsory finds its origin in a seventeenth-century French office book. It is drawn from the prophecies of Isaiah with a recurring refrain:

> **Pour down, O heavens, from above,**
> **and let the skies rain down righteousness.**
> *(Isaiah 45.8a)*

As such, it is a great expression of longing for the advent of Christ, summing up as it does the longings of the prophets for salvation and for the coming of the kingdom. The four verses are an eclectic assembly of texts:

1. Isaiah 64.9a, 10, 11a

2. Isaiah 64.6, 7

3. Isaiah 43.10a, 11, 13b

4. Isaiah 40.1a; 44.22a

There are a variety of musical settings available, and the Prose makes an effective introit, or a devotion in an Advent carol service, or it may be used as part of a penitential rite during the season.

Christmas in Advent

While the purists will resist any Christmas services before Christmas Eve, the fact is that society at large sees Christmas as an extended festival culminating in 25 December. The welcome fact is that people do flock to carol services in the lead up to Christmas, schools and colleges anticipate Christmas, the festive season is well into its swing even before Advent begins. This is a tension that we simply have to live with and seek to use creatively.

A number of things can be done. Most carol services or Christingles are held in the afternoon and early evening, not least so that candle imagery can be used to good effect. So it is possible to keep to an Advent discipline on the Sunday mornings in Advent; or in morning all-age services, for example, to use materials that are genuinely preparatory. An annual Jesse Tree service, where children have made the symbols and can decorate the tree with them, can strengthen the sense of looking forward to Christmas itself.

The Jesse Tree

At St Andrew's, the Junior Church had been preparing throughout the autumn programme for a Jesse Tree service to be held on the morning of Advent 4. Each week, the children learned about Old Testament characters who help us to understand the meaning of the coming of Jesus. For each character, the children made brightly coloured symbols (for example, an ark for Noah, a burning bush for Moses, a harp for King David) to decorate their own tree, and a much bigger symbol to decorate the church Christmas tree. In mid-December, two members of the church cut down branches of willow, one for each child, sprayed them with silver paint and made firm bases for them with plaster of Paris. On Advent 4, the children decorated their trees in the hall before the service. There was then a great procession into church, the forty trees filling every window ledge, and the service began. At the appropriate moment, the large symbols were hung on the Christmas tree, bare except for Christmas lights, which were not yet switched on. (To make sure that everyone enjoyed the experience and to maintain a degree of order, each child had an adult 'minder'.) The service proceeded as follows:

Greeting and welcome

Hymn: 'Hark the glad sound'

Opening prayer, penitential kyrie confession and absolution, and the Lord's Prayer

Reading: Isaiah 11.1–3

Symbols of Adam, Eve and Noah

   Song about Noah

Symbols of Abraham, Jacob and Joseph

   Hymn: 'As Jacob with travel was weary one day'

Symbol of Moses

   Song: 'How great is our God'

Symbols of King David and King Solomon

   Solo: Spiritual: 'Little David, play on your harp'

Symbol of the prophet Isaiah

Prayers

Hymn: 'Long ago, prophets knew'

Gospel reading for Advent 4

> Symbols of Joseph, Mary, and Jesus
>
> Switching on of the church Christmas tree lights
>
> Carol: 'Once in royal David's city', during which the Jesse Trees are presented to the children
>
> Blessing

Many churches will wish to hold a carol service on Advent 4, perhaps incorporating a children's nativity; at least on Advent 4 the annunciation stories are prominent. But the advice is surely sound that we should hold some things back for Christmas Eve/Day: the white or gold liturgical colour, the change of the candles in the Advent Wreath to white or gold, the placing of the Christ-child in the crib, the great concluding verse to 'Adeste, fideles', 'Yea, Lord, we greet thee'.

'Darkness to light' imagery

There are a number of ways in which the theme of 'darkness to light' can be illustrated dramatically:

* Members of the congregation can be given individual candles. These should be 9–12 inches long with drip cards (some church requisites companies advertise these as 'Easter Vigil candles', i.e. candles large enough to sustain an extended period of readings). The service begins in darkness; the Advent Wreath or a large candle is lit at the beginning and the congregational candles are then lit by passing the light along the rows. The candlelight can be supplemented where necessary by selective electric lights.

* Candles (congregational and on specially devised candle stands) are lit gradually, from west to east. Again, the service begins in darkness; the ministers at the west end light the Advent Wreath or a large candle. If there are six readings, for example, each reading is read from a station as the liturgical action moves eastwards e.g.

    Reading 1   The font

    Reading 2   West end of nave

Reading 3   East end of nave

Reading 4   Lectern

Reading 5   The chancel step

Reading 6   The altar.

As each reading is proclaimed, the candles around that area of the church are lit, so that gradually the church fills with candlelight. Some electric lighting will be needed for congregational carols and any responses; however, the effect is not lost if electric lighting is phased in and out with care.

• The choir and ministers may carry candles, but the church electric lights are used, beginning with darkness and gradually increasing the degree of light through the service. If a church has dimmer switches, they come into their own here. Where Revelation 21. 22–22.5 is used as the final lesson, the raising of the lights to full intensity can be very dramatic and moving.

• Where the congregation is not vast and there is plenty of space, the whole congregation, carrying candles, can move eastwards, using seating at various points in the church, e.g. west end, mid-nave, front-nave, chancel, sanctuary.

4 Christmas Season

What sweeter music can we bring
Than a carol, for to sing
The birth of this our heav'nly King?
Awake the voice! Awake the string:

Dark and dull night, fly hence away,
And give the honour to this day,
That sees December turn to May,
If we ask the reason, say:

We see him come, and know him ours,
Who with his sunshine and his showers
Turns all the patient ground to flowers.

Robert Herrick

Jagged edges

The last chapter concluded with the note of realism that Christmas is increasingly anticipated during the second half of Advent. Therefore, in many places much of the material in the Christmas section of *Times and Seasons* will be used earlier than Christmas Day itself.

However, the Christmas season has an integrity of its own, and wise liturgical planning will seek to honour this. Indeed, so much pre-Christmas worship is organized with the needs of the casual worshipper in mind that there is a very good case for seeing the Christmas season and beyond as a creative opportunity for sustained reflection on the 'great and mighty wonder' of the mystery of the Incarnation in the life of the regular worshipping community itself.

Christmas in context

There are two primary cycles of the Christian Year; the Easter cycle and the Christmas cycle. The Easter cycle begins with the preparatory season of Lent, embracing Holy Week and the paschal *triduum* or three days' celebration of the dying and rising of Jesus, but then extends through Eastertide and incorporates the Ascension before coming to glorious completion on the Day of Pentecost. The Christmas cycle echoes this by including the preparatory season of Advent, the twelve days of Christmas, the season of Epiphany with its focus on the revelation of the Word made flesh to the Magi, in Jesus' baptism and in signs and wonders, and the concluding multi-faceted feast of Candlemas on 2 February.

So whereas the secular world sees Christmas ending on 25 December, in the Church it is only beginning as Christians learn to bow before the mystery of the coming of God into the world in Jesus Christ. The material in *Times and Seasons* for this whole period is designed to assist such reflection.

The Twelve Days of Christmas

Or perhaps, the thirteen, as in many churches it is Christmas Eve that sees the largest attendances and the greatest scope for creativity. The Christmas section includes material for carol services, crib and Christingle services, the principal Christmas Eucharist, and material for the New Year. *Common Worship: Festivals* includes resources for 'the Christmas Saints' (Stephen, John, and the Holy Innocents) and for 1 January, the Naming and Circumcision of Jesus.

The material assumes that as Christmas is a great festival, churches will think creatively about how church buildings are decorated and appointed. Among the possibilities are the following.

The crib The crib should ideally be erected in a prominent place in the church, both as an illustration of the Christmas story and as an aid to prayer and devotion. Traditionally, the figures of the Magi are not placed in the crib until Epiphany, although many ministers will incorporate them in a crib service simply because every school nativity includes them and carols and songs refer to them. However, the placing of Magi in different locations in the church, as it were on their journey, engages the imagination of children, who will look for them on each occasion they attend until they 'arrive' at the Epiphany.

The Christmas tree Most churches use a Christmas tree as part of decorating the church. When lit well, the tree can be a vivid sign of Christ the Light, while evergreens have long had associations with the bringing of salvation. In some churches, the tree is a focus of giving, both presents and money, for needy children and charities. A simple service for the lighting of a Christmas tree can be an effective start to Christmas celebrations, particularly when celebrated in late afternoon and linked to giving.

The Jesse Tree As a visible symbol of salvation history leading to the coming of Christ, the placing of Christmas symbols on the tree is a vital part of the meaning of the Jesse Tree. This is ideally done on Christmas Eve or Christmas Day itself and, along with the crib, can be a useful teaching medium. In some places the tree is also decorated with simple gifts to be distributed either to children or to the sick and housebound during the Christmas period.

The Advent Wreath The lighting of the 'King' or central white candle on Christmas Day also brings to completion what the lighting of the other candles symbolizes: the fulfilment of the longings of the Old Testament in the coming of Christ. There is a good case for changing all the candles to white or gold for Christmas Day as a sign of the coming of 'festival', and for lighting the candles throughout the Christmas season until the Epiphany or Candlemas.

Flowers and evergreens The tradition of banning flowers and other decorations in Advent was doubtless encouraged by a false equivalence of Advent with Lent. However, there is a good case, as stated above, for making the Advent Wreath *the* focus of decoration during Advent and then transforming the church building for Christmas. This is best done as part of a genuinely community activity.

Light While *The Promise of His Glory* stated that light symbolism can be grossly overdone, the increasing use of candles across all Christian traditions and as a central part of many 'secular' Christmases should encourage the church to think carefully about its symbolism and how it can help people connect. For example, if there is a spirituality of 'waiting for Christ', the careful use of subdued lighting before Christmas services helps create a sense of quiet anticipation and can encourage worshippers into a much more prayerful period of preparation before the start of Christmas services. It should also be remembered that in giving light, a candle gives of itself – a symbol perhaps both of God's self-giving in Christ and the call and cost of discipleship.

The lectionary

Three sets of readings are provided for Christmas Night and Christmas Day; any set may be used, but a note states that set III should be used at some point during the celebration. It has been customary in the Roman Catholic tradition to celebrate three Christmas masses: at night, at dawn, and during the day, but this is partly in imitation of the papal practice of celebrating one mass at three *different* churches in Rome.

The sets of readings are as follows:

I	Isaiah 9.2–7	The people who walked in darkness have seen a great light
	Psalm 96	Tell of his salvation from day to day
	Titus 2.11–14	The grace of God has appeared
	Luke 2.1–14 (15–20)	The birth of Jesus, angels and shepherds.
II	Isaiah 62.6–12	See, your salvation comes
	Psalm 97	All the peoples behold his glory
	Titus 3.4–7	When the goodness and loving-kindness of God our Saviour appeared, he saved us
	Luke 2.(1–7), 8–20	Angels and shepherds.
III	Isaiah 52.7–10	They see the return of the Lord to Zion
	Psalm 98	Let the hills sing together for joy at the presence of the Lord
	Hebrews 1.1–4 (5–12)	God has spoken to us by a Son
	John 1.1–14	The Word was made flesh and dwelt among us.

However, at the principal Eucharist, John 1.1–14 may be read as a dismissal Gospel, pre-supposing that one of the Lukan Gospels has been read earlier.

The lectionary for the First Sunday of Christmas sets Gospel readings from the infancy narratives, enabling Anglicans to follow the Roman Catholic practice of remembering 'the Holy Family':

A	Matthew 2.13–23	The flight into Egypt, the slaughter of the Innocents, the settlement at Nazareth
B	Luke 2.15–21	The shepherds visit the manger, the circumcision and naming of Jesus
C	Luke 2.41–52	Jesus as a boy in the Temple at Jerusalem.

Although it rarely falls, the Second Sunday of Christmas is provided with one set of readings; the Gospel is the complete Johannine prologue (John 1.1–18).

We turn now to the *Times and Seasons* provision.

Seasonal material

The seasonal resources draw on rich veins of biblical imagery and association from both Old and New Testaments; these may profitably be traced in teaching.

Invitations to confession The first text takes up the theme of the annunciation to Joseph from St Matthew's Gospel (an important reference, as the role of Joseph is often overlooked); the other two texts are written specifically for use either during the night or in the daytime, taking up the theme of light. The reference to the 'sun of righteousness' (Malachi 4.2) recalls the recent winter solstice, the rising of Christ, the true 'sun of righteousness', the dayspring.

Kyrie Confessions Two forms are provided, the first consciously Trinitarian, the second drawing on aspects of the Christmas story.

Absolutions Two texts drawn from the *Main Volume*, the first alluding to John 1.14 and the second to John 3.16.

Gospel Acclamation From the *Main Volume*, again from John 1.14.

Intercessions Five forms of prayer are provided. The first and the fifth are brief forms of prayer to Jesus, the latter providing a structure to incorporate simple biddings; both would be suitable for all-age services. The second set repeats the phrase 'on this holy night' and skilfully links aspects of the Christmas story with areas for intercession. It is intended for use on Christmas Eve during the night, but a note allows adaptation for other occasions. The third and fourth forms both draw on the titles of Isaiah 9 ('Wonderful Counsellor, Mighty God . . .', etc.) but with one important difference. The first of the two forms is a prayer to the Father, while the second is a prayer to Christ.

Introductions to the Peace The first draws on Isaiah 9.6 from the *Main Volume*, the second on Luke 2.14, a reprise of the beginning of Gloria in excelsis.

Prayer at the Preparation of the Table A new prayer, skilfully alluding to 2 Corinthians 8.9 and the invocation of the Spirit in the eucharistic prayer.

> Word made flesh, life of the world,
> in your incarnation you embraced our poverty:
> by your Spirit may we share in your riches.
> **Amen.**

Prefaces Six short prefaces are provided, the first from the seasonal resources of the *Main Volume*, four from the *President's Edition*, and one from *New Patterns*. The short preface for the Holy Family is particularly suitable for Christmas 1.

Extended Preface From the *Main Volume*, based on the Christmas preface from the Roman *Sacramentary*.

Blessings and Endings Three 'short' blessings and one extended or solemn blessing are provided, the last being suitable for principal celebrations.

Acclamations Six sets are provided, drawing on Isaiah 9.2, 6; Luke 1.68; Psalm 97.11; 1 John 1.1–3, 8; 1 John 3.1; Psalm 2.7, John 1.12; 1 Timothy 3.16; John 1.14.

Short Passages of Scripture Five texts are given: the first two are suitable as introductory sentences; the last three may profitably be used as offertory or post-communion sentences, or at the conclusion of a Service of the Word. The fourth sentence:

> And the Word was made flesh and dwelt among us,
> and we beheld his glory.

could be used as a repeated refrain throughout an act of worship, or as a response to Bible readings.

The Eucharist of Christmas Night or Morning

This is the only fully worked-out service in the Christmas section of *Times and Seasons*. Again, this is not to limit creativity but to provide a model capable of local adaptation. One of the main historic differences between the Easter cycle and the Christmas cycle in the Western Church is that the latter is a more diffuse cycle; however, the tradition of an evening First Communion of Christmas, 'Midnight Mass', or Christmas morning celebration is prevalent and a common approach strengthens Anglican liturgical identity. The essential form is Order 1 with the full range of seasonal proper material. However, there are some distinctive features.

The Gathering

The rite makes provision for a procession to the crib; this could include the whole congregation if space allows. A congregational carol begins the rite; the principal ministers gather at the crib and the president may place the bambino in the crib. Words from the seventeenth-century writer Richard Crashaw or a responsory drawn from David Silk's *Prayers for Use at the Alternative Services* may be used, followed by the greeting and possibly words of welcome and introduction. The crib is then blessed, and the prayers of penitence are said at the crib, reflecting the fact that Jesus came to save us from our sins (Matthew 1.21). The ministers then proceed to the place where the ministry of the word is celebrated.

There are a number of musical possibilities. The opening carol can be split; for example, 'Once in Royal David's city' is appropriate, some verses being sung on the way to the crib and some in procession to the place for the Liturgy of the Word. 'O little Town' is another possibility for night services, particularly if the poignant, though often omitted, verse 'Where children pure and happy' is incorporated to make a five-verse hymn. On Christmas morning, 'Christians awake! Salute the happy morn', or 'See, amid the winter's snow' are particularly suitable. Alternatively, a sung Gloria in excelsis can be used for the procession from the crib.

Of course, in many churches the crib will have been blessed earlier, perhaps at a very well-attended Christmas Eve crib service in the early evening. If that is the case, it can still be appropriate and dramatic to

keep a station at the crib as part of the opening procession; the
following form could be used:

Processional Hymn

The congregation turns to face the crib.

President   'Do I not fill heaven and earth?' says the Lord.

All   **Now the Word is made flesh and laid in a
narrow manger.**

    From eternity to eternity you are God,

All   **and now we see you as a newborn child.**

President   From the Christ who is Immanuel, God with us,
grace, light and peace be with you

All   **and also with you.**

The President welcomes the congregation.

President   Dear friends, as we meet to celebrate the birth of
Christ, let us pray that God will bless this crib, that
all who worship his Son, born of the Virgin Mary,
may come to share his life in glory.

    We pray you, Lord, to purify our hearts
that they may be worthy to become your
    dwelling-place.
Let us never fail to find room for you,
but come and abide in us,
that we also may abide in you,
for as at this time you were born into the
    world for us,
and live and reign, King of kings and Lord of lords,
now and for ever.

All   **Amen.**

The prayers of penitence follow.

Processional Hymn (continued) or Gloria in excelsis.

Another variation is to carry the bambino in procession at the
beginning of the rite and place it on the holy table for the duration
of the Eucharist. At the end of the service, the bambino is placed in
the crib.

Gospel Acclamations

As well as the form based on John 1.14 from the *Main Volume*, a more developed form from *Promise* is included:

Today Christ is born:
alleluia.
Today the Saviour has come:
alleluia.
Today the angels sing on earth:
alleluia. Glory to God in the highest.

The text may be sung, although this is likely to diminish participation where there are many visitors. Perhaps the most effective use is to proclaim it loudly both before and after the Gospel.

Breaking of the Bread

This excellent text in *Promise*, drawn from the Anglican Church of Canada, is most effective and it also appears in the Epiphany section of *Times and Seasons* (p. 167) so that it can be used throughout the Incarnational period:

We break the bread of life,
and that life is the light of the world.
God here among us,
light in the midst of us,
bring us to light and life.

The Dismissal

Provision is made for a dismissal Gospel, before or after the blessing. This is the traditional 'Last Gospel' of the medieval mass, John 1.1–14. If this option is chosen, an alternative Gospel reading should be used at the Liturgy of the Word. Again, it can be effective if the dismissal Gospel is proclaimed from the crib. In more catholic traditions, it will be the custom to bow or genuflect at the words 'And the Word was made flesh and dwelt among us'. It invites us to proclaim by word and deed the 'Word made flesh', to proclaim him as the true light, as we seek, in and with Christ and by the power of his Spirit, to continue his healing and reconciling work today.

Carol services in the Christmas season

As with the Advent carol service, resources are provided which recognize that there are many different approaches to carol services depending on the occasion, musical resources and setting.

Three forms of Bidding Prayers and Introduction are given. The first is the well-loved form by Eric Milner-White, a classic bidding prayer, followed by the Lord's Prayer and concluding benediction. This presupposes that other prayers within the service will be minimal. The second, adapted from David Silk, is also a bidding prayer concluding with the Lord's Prayer but cast in more contemporary idiom. The third is an introduction, with silence and the Collect for Christmas Eve; this presupposes that other forms of prayer will be used in the service.

Whichever form is used, a rubric suggests that an acclamation and blessing should conclude the service.

Three sequences of readings are provided:

Good news for the poor
Old Testament lections with accompanying psalmody
Philippians 2.5–11
Gospel canticle: Magnificat

Gospel reading: Luke 1.26–38 (Advent)
　　　　　　　　Luke 2.1–20 (Christmas)

The Gospel of Luke
The entire Lukan infancy narrative
Gospel canticle: Benedictus *or* Magnificat *or* Nunc dimittis
Titus 2.11–14; 3.3–7

The King's College pattern
The traditional sequence of readings from the Fall to the Incarnation, including the coming of the Magi and the ninth lesson: the Johannine Prologue.

Again, these merely provide models. For many churches, nine lessons will be too many; carol services may incorporate drama or a nativity play, when two or three readings may be sufficient. Some churches now use religious poetry and readings along with Bible readings.

Also, the above examples are not exhaustive. An instance of creative adaptation of the Milner-White sequence is evident at Durham Cathedral, a pattern using wisdom Christology.

Jesus Christ, the Power of God and the Wisdom of God

The queen of the South will rise at the judgement with the people of this generation and condemn them, because she came from the ends of the earth to listen to the wisdom of Solomon, and see, something greater than Solomon is here.
Luke 11.31

He himself is before all things, and in him all things hold together. *Colossians 1.17*

1. Wisdom proclaims her presence with God in creation from the beginning *Proverbs 8.22–30*

2. King Solomon prays for the gift of wisdom
   Wisdom of Solomon 9.1–4, 10–13, 14a, 16–17

3. The prophet foretells the coming of a king on whom rests the spirit of wisdom and understanding *Isaiah 10.33–11.6*

4. The angel Gabriel greets Mary with the promise of a son who shall be king *Luke 1.26–35, 38*

5. St Luke tells of the birth of Jesus *Luke 2.1–7*

6. Shepherds go to the manger *Luke 2.8–16*

7. Wise men from the East worship the Christ child
   Matthew 2.1–11

8. St Paul sets out the significance of Christ in creation and redemption *Colossians 1.15–20*

9. St John unfolds the great mystery of the Incarnation
   John 1.1–14

Christingle services and crib services

Again, rather than fully worked out services, *Times and Seasons* provides two structures with accompanying resource material. This recognizes that the approach to such services is largely determined by local tradition and resources and the age range of those present. Many other resources are also available, not least from the Children's Society in the case of the Christingle. Moreover, the Christingle imagery is sufficiently broad for creative use in Advent, Epiphany or at Candlemas. Both patterns focus on the telling of the story, leading into praise, thanksgiving and prayer. It is suggested that for the thanksgiving, the lighting of a large candle, or Christingle, or the candles of the Advent Wreath will provide a useful focus.

The outlines are as follows:

A Christingle Service

- Greeting

- Lighting of a Candle

- Thanksgiving

- Ministry of the Word
  Reading
  Talk or Address

- Offering of Gifts

- Prayers

- The Lord's Prayer

- Lighting/Presentation of Christingles

- Ending/Blessing

A Crib Service

- Greeting

- Lighting of a Candle

- Penitential Section

- Collect

- Ministry of the Word
  Reading
  Building up of Crib while Telling the Story
  Talk or Address

- Thanksgiving

- Prayers

- The Lord's Prayer

- Ending/Blessing

Useful resources are provided to clothe the skeleton services. For example, at the lighting of the candle at the beginning of the service:

Today we remember Jesus and the story of his birth;
Jesus is our King.

As a candle is lit

Jesus Christ is the light of the world;
Jesus is our Way.

With Jesus even dark places are light;
Jesus is the Truth.

In Jesus we shall live for ever:
Jesus is our Life.

A prayer of confession is suggested for use with small children:

Father God,
we are sorry
for the things we do and say and think
which make you sad,
and for not thinking of others
before ourselves.
Please forgive us,
and help us to love you and other people
more and more.
Amen.

A wide variety of simple responsive material is provided, while other resources, e.g. the simple forms of intercession in the earlier Seasonal Material section, could profitably be drawn upon.

Additional prayers for use at Christmastide

This section provides two forms for the blessing of the crib: the first form is the one incorporated into the Eucharist of Christmas Night or Morning. The second is adapted from Eric Milner-White.

> In the faith of Christ,
> and in your name, O God most holy,
> we hallow this crib of Christmas,
> to set before the eyes of your children
> the great love and humility
> of Jesus Christ your only Son;
> who for us, and for our salvation,
> came down as at this time from heaven,
> and was incarnate by the Holy Spirit
> of the Virgin Mary his mother,
> and was made man;
> to whom with you and the same Spirit
> be all honour, majesty, glory and worship,
> now and to the ages of ages.
> **Amen.**

Five 'Prayers at the crib' are then given, drawing on material in *Promise*, which could be used in Christmastide or Epiphanytide. One possibility would be to make a prayer at the crib a focus on each Sunday throughout the Christmas–Epiphany seasons, either at the beginning of worship (as part of an entrance procession) or at the conclusion of worship.

Resource material for the beginning of a new year

Since the Millennium, the tradition of services to mark the beginning of the new calendar year has undergone something of a revival, including ecumenical initiatives. This has built on ecumenical material provided for the Millennium celebrations. *Times and Seasons* has collated material from *Promise* and *New Patterns*, providing flexible resources for eucharistic or non-eucharistic worship. This includes some resonant acclamations:

Jesus, Lord of time,
hold us in your eternity.

Jesus, image of God,
travel with us the life of faith.

Jesus, friend of sinners,
heal the brokenness of our world.

Jesus, Lord of tomorrow,
draw us into your future. Amen.

or

A thousand years in God's sight are like a single day.
Like an evening that has already gone.

Christ is the first and the last,
the beginning and the end.

Jesus stands at the door and knocks.
Lord Jesus, enter our homes and our lives.

You hold the key to God's way of justice,
Open to us your kingdom of peace.

The renewal of the Covenant

One particular feature of the material is the incorporation of part of the Methodist Covenant Service, traditionally celebrated at or near the beginning of the New Year. The Covenant Service owes its origin to John Wesley's adaptation of material from seventeenth-century Puritan sources. The material in *Times and Seasons* uses the heart of the service as found in *The Methodist Worship Book* (1999). Two forms of the renewal of the covenant are found there: the first (p. 110) is the traditional form stretching back to Wesley and including the (for some) controversial words 'put me to suffering'. The more contemporary form runs as follows:

Eternal God,
in your faithful and enduring love
you call us to share in your gracious covenant in Jesus Christ.
In obedience we hear and accept your commands;
in love we seek to do your perfect will;
with joy we offer ourselves anew to you.
We are no longer our own but yours.

I am no longer my own but yours.
Your will, not mine, be done in all things,
wherever you may place me,
in all that I do and in all that I may endure;
when there is work for me and when there is none;
when I am troubled and when I am at peace.
Your will be done
when I am valued and when I am disregarded;
when I find fulfilment and when it is lacking;
when I have all things and when I have nothing.
I willingly offer all that I have and am
to serve you, as and where you choose.
Glorious and blessed God,
Father, Son and Holy Spirit,
you are mine and I am yours.
May it be so for ever.
Let this covenant now made on earth
be fulfilled in heaven.   Amen.

Of course, Anglicans may use the Methodist Covenant Service in its entirety, and this is particularly appropriate in creative local ecumenical partnerships.

Common Worship: Festivals

Common Worship: Festivals provides resource material for the four festivals falling within Christmastide:

Stephen, Deacon, First Martyr	26 December
John, Apostle and Evangelist	27 December
The Holy Innocents	28 December
The Naming and Circumcision of Jesus	1 January

Suitable material may also be adapted from the provision for the following festivals during the year:

Joseph of Nazareth	19 March
The Annunciation of Our Lord to the Blessed Virgin Mary	25 March
The Visit of the Blessed Virgin Mary to Elizabeth	31 May
The Birth of John the Baptist	24 June
Common of the Blessed Virgin Mary	

'The Christmas Saints'

Stephen, John and the Holy Innocents, traditionally known as 'the Christmas saints' or 'companions of Christ' (*Comites Christi*), are often overlooked in post-Christmas collapse! However, the *Common Worship* lectionary makes provision for these feasts, when falling on a Sunday, to replace the provision for the First Sunday of Christmas, and each one in its own way resonates with the story of Christmas. But where these festivals fall on a weekday, and quiet post-Christmas recollection is valued, the rich material provided here gives scope for sensitive and creative celebration.

The Feast of Stephen underlines the truth that Christ came down to earth to embrace human suffering; so the form of intercession begins:

> Incarnate Lord,
> you came down to earth from heaven
>   to embrace the pain and sorrows of our sinful world, . . .

and goes on to pray for all who are persecuted for the cause of truth, all who exercise authority as political or religious leaders, and all who use violence to silence their opponents. It then prays for constancy in witnessing to the truth and following Christ, for all those for whom the joy of this season is overshadowed by pain, grief, or failure; and in commemoration of all who have gone before us in faith.

The material for John draws especially on the Fourth Gospel, on the titles given to Christ in that Gospel and, in the Intercessions, on the 'I am' sayings. The extended preface summarizes these truths:

All glory and honour be yours always and everywhere,
mighty creator, ever-living God,
through Jesus Christ our Lord;
for he is the Word before all creation,
the Life made manifest,
the Light who shines in the darkness.
He is the Living Bread who has come down from heaven,
the Good Shepherd, who lays down his life for the sheep,
the Lamb of God who takes away the sin of the world.
He stands among us in his risen power,
and shows us his hands and his side.
With joy we worship him as our Lord and our God.
Therefore with all the angels of heaven
we lift our voices to proclaim the glory of your name
and sing our joyful hymn of praise:

The Holy Innocents material reflects on human cruelty and especially on the loss of children, a pastoral reality felt most acutely in the Christmas season by bereaved families. The form of intercession (see Festivals in GS 1549, p. 44) in particular, gives short biddings suggesting the use of silence:

In peace let us pray to the God of love.

Righteous God,
your Son our Saviour Jesus Christ dwelt among us and shared
    our grief and our pain.

We pray for the children of our world,
that they may grow up knowing love and security.

We pray for all children who suffer physical or mental abuse.

We pray for all communities in our world
who live with the memories of massacre and gross cruelty.

We pray for parents and guardians that they may be given grace
to care for the children entrusted to them.

We pray for all who are corrupted by power
and who regard human life as cheap.

We pray for parents who have suffered the death of a child.

As we celebrate the coming of the Christ-child,
we rejoice in the fellowship of the Holy Innocents
and commit the children of this community,
our nation and our world to you,
our righteous God.

Merciful Father,
accept these prayers
for the sake of your Son,
our Saviour Jesus Christ.

The Naming and Circumcision of Jesus

This feast, the old octave day of Christmas, is a solemnity of Mary, the Mother of the Lord, in the modern Roman calendar. *Common Worship* follows the Prayer Book and the old Roman tradition of observing the naming and circumcision on the eighth day after the birth (Luke 2.21). The material concentrates on the Holy Name of Jesus, including a form of intercession using verses from the hymn 'How sweet the name of Jesus sounds' as refrains, which of course may be sung.

The extended preface (see Festivals in GS 1549, p. 5), a new composition, reflects the insight, found in the Patristic Fathers, that the rite of circumcision foreshadowed the pouring out of the blood of Christ on the cross, as he who fulfils the law is obedient to the law for us. It also alludes to Christian baptism, recalling Colossians 2.11–15:

All glory and honour be yours always and everywhere,
mighty creator, ever-living God,
through Jesus Christ our Lord.
We praise you that on the eighth day
he was circumcised in obedience to the law of Moses,
that he might fulfil the law and reveal to us your grace and truth.
For here is foreshadowed
his perfect self-offering upon the cross,
the shedding of his blood to set us free from sin and death.
In baptism we die with him and are raised in him,
that we might walk in newness of life,
and proclaim the wonders of his saving name.
Therefore with all the angels of heaven
we lift our voices to proclaim the glory of your name
and sing our joyful hymn of praise:

5 Epiphany Season

> For these three miracles this great day we celebrate:
> on this day a star led the wise men to the crib:
> on this day wine was made from water at the wedding-feast:
> on this day Jesus came willingly to John to be baptized,
> so as to save us all. Alleluia.
>
> *From the old Roman evening office*

After Twelfth Night

The Christmas decorations are packed away for another year, cards are taken down, cheery wreaths removed from front doors, and there are January and February to face and, for many, Christmas to pay for! No wonder the Epiphany has struggled to make an impact; not many feel like celebrating the day after Twelfth Night. But this betrays a weakness in the western tradition, as exemplified by the Prayer Book – to see the Epiphany as a 'one-off', an annual remembrance of the coming of the Magi or, as the Prayer Book secondary title expresses it, 'the manifestation of Christ to the Gentiles'.

There is an older tradition of a much broader approach that extends far beyond the crib, which is characteristic of the Eastern Churches and not entirely absent from the western tradition, as the quotation above illustrates.

Manifesting glory

In Scripture, the manifestation of the Son of God, the Word made flesh, embraces a whole series of events: yes, there is the revelation by the angel to the shepherds; yes, there is the mysterious visit of Magi from the east, but there are also the resonant accounts of Jesus' baptism at the Jordan with the heavenly voice, 'You are/This is my Son'; and the great signs of the Fourth Gospel, the changing of water into wine and the power to heal and restore, the astounding claim to forgive sins, the discovery of the disciples that 'we have found the

Messiah' (John 1.41). Epiphany as a season, extending from 6 January to Candlemas on 2 February, gives an extended period of reflection on what the Incarnation means and how the reality of God among us was discerned and responded to.

No ordinary time

In the *ASB* calendar, Sundays were designated Sundays *after* Epiphany, and while the Sunday following the Epiphany was appointed 'The Baptism of Christ' and its liturgical colour was white, from the following Monday vestments and hangings returned to 'ordinary' green. *Common Worship* has redesignated the Sundays as Sundays *of* Epiphany, and the whole season is a white 'festal' season, so that the Christmas–Epiphany sequence is an extended celebration of the Incarnation lasting forty days and culminating in Candlemas, or the Presentation of Christ in the Temple, which historically took place forty days after birth according to Jewish custom. Of course, our use of liturgical time is sophisticated; this is not a simple chronology. We see Jesus in these weeks as a new-born infant, a child, a thirty-year-old man, and finally back as an infant; the point is that his manifestation was episodic and over time – but each episode is important for the whole.

Keeping festival

As well as festal hangings and vestments (where they are used), it is worth considering how some symbols can assist in giving a sense of unity to the season. While custom perhaps dictates that Christmas trees are removed after the Twelve Days of Christmas, the crib at least should stay as a focus for the whole incarnational cycle. Some churches retain the Advent Wreath and Jesse Tree (which often has symbols of the Magi, Baptism and Cana wedding feast), while banners and festal flowers keep the sense of celebration.

The scope of the season

The *Common Worship* calendar allows the Epiphany itself to be kept either on 6 January or on the Sunday preceding 6 January. The latter, of course, would bring the Epiphany into Christmastide, which simply underlines the interconnectedness of these two seasons. But the Epiphany Season has a number of important aspects:

6 January (or Sunday preceding)	The Epiphany: the visit of the Magi; Jesus revealed to Gentiles from the East
Sunday after 6 January	The Baptism of Christ: Jesus revealed as the Son of God
18–25 January	The Week of Prayer for Christian Unity
25 January	The Conversion of Paul
2 February	The Presentation of Christ in the Temple (or Candlemas): Jesus revealed to Simeon and Anna.

Unity and mission form part of the backcloth to the season. The Week of Prayer for Christian Unity is well established in Britain, extending from the Roman Catholic commemoration of the Confession of St Peter (18 January) to the Feast of the Conversion of Paul (25 January). This itself has resonance: Christians unite in confession of Jesus as 'the Christ, the Son of the living God' (Matthew 16.16) and recognize the vocation of Peter as 'Apostle to the Jews' and Paul as 'Apostle to the Gentiles'. The Epiphany Gospel readings tell of the revealing of the true nature of Christ as people, including the first disciples, believe in him and follow him. So *Times and Seasons* provides rich resources for prayer for the unity of the Church and the mission of the Church.

The scope of the provision

In *Times and Seasons*, the following material is provided:

- Seasonal resource material

- Seasonal material connected with the Theme of Unity

- Seasonal material connected with the Theme of Mission

- The Eucharist on the Feast of the Epiphany

- The Eucharist on the Feast of the Baptism of Christ

- A Service for the Festival of the Baptism of Christ

- The Eucharist on the Feast of the Presentation of Christ in the Temple

Other material can be drawn in. In *Common Worship: Christian Initiation*, seasonal material is provided for baptisms in Epiphanytide (pp. 150–55), while a full range of resources for the Conversion of Paul (25 January) is found in *Common Worship: Festivals*.

Seasonal material

Three sets of seasonal material are provided: for the Epiphany season, for unity and for mission. Some of this is interchangeable, and as the Epiphany season progresses, daily and Sunday worship may well reflect one or more of these great themes.

Epiphany season

Some of the resources here are specific to the Feast of the Epiphany, the Baptism of Christ or Candlemas. Other material is more general, drawing on the major theme of the revealing of God among us.

Invitations to Confession Three forms are provided: the first from the *Main Volume*; the second specific to the Baptism of Christ, drawing on Titus 3.4, 5; and the third adapted from Romans 12.1 (self-offering).

Kyrie Confessions The four forms are suitable throughout the season: the first is based on Psalm 67; the second on titles of Christ; the third on themes of new life, restoration, and unity in the Spirit; and the fourth asks for inward illumination, the opening of eyes and unstopping of ears, alluding to gospel healing narratives.

Gospel Acclamations Specific texts are provided for the Epiphany, Baptism of Christ and Candlemas as well as the *Main Volume* seasonal text.

Intercessions Five texts are given: the first is suitable for Epiphany, drawing on the Matthean account; the second is an intercession for the life and renewal of the Church; the third reflects the theme of mission; the fourth is for the Baptism of Christ; and the fifth is for Candlemas.

Introductions to the Peace Two seasonal texts are supplemented by texts proper to the Baptism of Christ and Candlemas.

Prayers at the Preparation of the Table Four prayers are included, two of which are adapted from Anglican use in Canada and New Zealand. The second text runs:

> Lord, accept your people's gifts,
> not gold, frankincense or myrrh,
> but hearts and voices raised in praise
> of Jesus Christ, our light and our salvation.

Prefaces A comprehensive collection of ten texts from various sources.

Extended Prefaces Three prefaces, two drawn from the *Main Volume* and one from *Promise*.

Blessings One form of extended blessing is from the *President's Edition*; the short blessings are drawn from the *Main Volume, President's Edition* and *New Patterns*. One form for the Presentation is from the Church Mission Society and the Church in Wales:

> Keep your eyes fixed on Jesus, who was wounded for our sins,
> that you may bear in your life the love and joy and peace
> which are the marks of Jesus in his disciples;
> and the blessing . . .

Short Passages of Scripture Nine texts are provided, two of which are specific to the Baptism of Christ.

Seasonal material connected with the theme of Unity

This section provides parallel material to that of the main seasonal material, but with some additions. The resources here can be used as part of a local church's regular prayer or for the constructing of ecumenical services, complementing material produced annually by Churches Together in Britain and Ireland. Some of the material in the Reconciliation and Restoration section of *Common Worship: Christian Initiation* (pp. 240–63) is easily adapted for unity week.

In particular, *Times and Seasons* provides additional penitential material, in the form of an act of confession:

Most merciful God
we confess that we have sinned against you
and against one another,
in thought, and word, and deed.
We are truly sorry for our pride,
and for our lack of faith, of understanding and of love.
We repent of our narrow-mindedness,
of our bitterness and our prejudices.
Pardon and forgive us,
save us and renew us,
that we may delight in your will and walk in your
  ways;
through Jesus Christ our Lord.
Amen.

a more extended penitential rite, recalling our common baptism, with sprinkling of baptismal water:

O God, the Father of our Lord Jesus Christ,
our only Saviour, the Prince of peace:
give us grace seriously to lay to heart
the great dangers we are in by our unhappy divisions.
We confess our hatred and prejudice
and all else that hinders us from godly union and concord.
As there is but one body and one Spirit,
and one hope of our calling,
one Lord, one faith, one baptism,
one God and Father of us all,
so may we henceforth be all of one heart and soul,
united in one holy bond of truth and peace,
of faith and charity,
and with one mouth give you glory;
through Jesus Christ our Lord.

The president prays over a vessel of water

God our Father,
your gift of water brings life and freshness to the earth;
in baptism it is a sign of the washing away of our sins
and the gift of life eternal.

Sanctify this water, we pray:
renew the living spring of your life within us,
that we may be free from sin
and filled with your saving health;
through Christ our Lord.
Amen.

The president and people are sprinkled.
Meanwhile suitable anthems may be sung.

The president concludes

May almighty God cleanse us from sin
and make us worthy of the kingdom of his glory.
Amen.

The Extended Preface is adapted from ICEL (the Roman Catholic International Commission on English in the Liturgy) and is a good example of creative writing.

Father, all-powerful and ever-living God,
we do well always and everywhere to give you thanks
through Jesus Christ our Lord.
By him, your only Son,
who restored to us peace through the blood of his cross,
you willed to reconcile all creatures.
In him you have led us to the knowledge of your truth,
that bound together by one faith and one baptism
we might become his body.
Through him you have given your Holy Spirit to all peoples
to work marvels by innumerable gifts
and an abundant variety of graces.
Gathering us together in unity,
your Spirit dwells in the hearts of all your children,
filling the whole Church with his presence
and guiding it with wisdom from above.
And so, with steadfast love,
we proclaim your glory
and join with hosts of angels
in their triumphant hymn of praise:

A form of extended Dismissal is provided, incorporating an acclamation:

> There is one body and one spirit.
> **There is one hope to which we were called;**
> one Lord, one faith, one baptism,
> **one God and Father of all**.

followed by a dismissal Gospel (John 17.21b–23 or John 10.14–16), a blessing invoking the unity in diversity of the Trinity:

> May God the Father, Son, and Holy Spirit,
> three persons in one God,
> inspire you to live as one,
> that you may witness to the perfect unity of his love;
> and the blessing . . .

and dismissal:

> One in heart and one in mind,
> and empowered by the Spirit,
> go in the peace of Christ.
> **In the name of Christ.   Amen**.

Seasonal material connected with the theme of Mission

The full range of material from *The Promise of His Glory* is reproduced here and of course may be used whenever a church is engaging with issues of mission throughout the year. The extended eucharistic preface is a creative transposition of material from the Letter to the Ephesians, and a new dismissal rite, drawing on *New Patterns*, has the following sequence:

O Lord, open my lips
and my mouth shall proclaim your praise.

When we were still helpless
Christ died for the ungodly.

The proof of God's amazing love is this:
while we were still sinners, Christ died for us.

Gospel Reading: Matthew 28.19–20 or John 20.21–22

Extended Blessing

The Dismissal: The Lord says, 'Go into all the world
and make disciples of all the nations'.
Go in the peace of Christ.
Thanks be to God.

The Eucharist on the Feast of the Epiphany

As with the fully worked out Eucharist for Christmas, this order includes a full selection of appropriate seasonal material. For example, from *New Patterns* it employs a form of Kyrie Confession based on Psalm 67: 'May your ways be known on the earth, your saving power among the nations', and a creative form of intercession based on the coming of the Wise Men.

There are two important distinctive features. The first is a presentation of gifts at the crib. In the order, it is suggested that this takes place at the Gospel. It could be done in the following way.

At St Margaret's, three older children are chosen each year for the Epiphany Eucharist. They have outgrown the Christmas children's nativity, but this service is very different and there are plenty of volunteers to be the 'three kings'. Elaborate costumes have been made, and highly decorated containers for the three gifts: for gold, old coins have been carefully polished and placed in a velvet-lined box; for frankincense, grains of incense are also piled into a handsome container; for myrrh, the oil of healing is used in an elegant glass decanter. At the entrance procession, the 'kings' enter with the ministers, but break off from the procession and begin a stately journey around the church building while the service begins.

During the hymn before the Gospel, they are seen walking from the east end of the church to the crib, placed at the west end near the font. The congregation follows the 'kings', and the ministers, one of them carrying the Gospel book, follow until all are standing around the crib.

A minister reads the Gospel from beside the crib. The president then raises his arms in prayer as, one by one, the 'three kings' approach the crib, kneel and present their gifts.

> *At the offering of gold*
> Blessed are you, Lord our God, King of the Universe:
> to you be praise and glory for ever!
> As gold in a furnace is tried
> and purified seven times in the fire,
> so purify our hearts and minds
> that we may be a royal priesthood
> acceptable in the service of your kingdom.

All **Blessed be God for ever.**

> *At the offering of incense*
> Blessed are you, Lord our God, King of the Universe:
> to you be praise and glory for ever!
> As our prayer rises before you as incense,
> so may we be presented before you
> with penitent hearts and uplifted hands
> to offer ourselves in your priestly service.

All **Blessed be God for ever.**

At the offering of myrrh
> Blessed are you, Lord our God, King of the Universe:
> to you be praise and glory for ever!
> As you give medicine to heal our sickness
> and the leaves of the trees for the healing of the nations,
> so anoint us with your healing power
> that we may be the first fruits of your new creation.

All **Blessed be God for ever.**

107

When all three gifts have been presented, the congregation keeps some moments of silence so that all can worship the king of the nations. The president gives a short address, the intercessions are led from the crib, and then the whole procession moves eastwards, singing a joyful hymn as the 'kings' lead the congregation to the place where the communion is celebrated. After the service, there is an Epiphany party.

Of course, there are other possibilities. The rubrics suggest that instead of gifts, the figures of the wise men could be placed in the crib by members of the congregation. Or the gifts could be offered at the beginning of the service, or after the Peace. A lot depends on the size of the building and the position of the crib.

There is also an extended rite of dismissal, which draws on the words of the Nunc dimittis, Christ as the Light to lighten the Gentiles, so anticipating the end of the Epiphany season at the beginning:

Blessed are you, Lord our God, King of the universe.
To you be glory and praise for ever.

From the rising of the sun to its setting
your name is proclaimed in all the world.
To you be glory and praise for ever.

When the time had fully come
you sent the Sun of Righteousness.
In him the fullness of your glory dwells.
To you be glory and praise for ever.

Gospel Reading: Luke 2.28–32
Extended Blessing

Dismissal: Christ is revealed to all creation.
Go in his peace.
Thanks be to God.

The Eucharist on the Festival of the Baptism of Christ

As we have already stated, in *Common Worship* there is some encouragement for churches to consider a variety of baptismal seasons, most notably Easter, Pentecost, All Saints and Epiphany. Epiphany is an obvious candidate because of the Sunday designated for the Baptism of Christ. This has the advantage of focusing on one or more of the many baptismal images found in Scripture. If 'dying and rising with Christ' is central to Easter spirituality, then on the Feast of the Baptism of Christ the following themes are prominent:

- becoming sons and daughters of God: 'You are my Son, the Beloved; with you I am well pleased';

- receiving the Holy Spirit: 'the Spirit descending like a dove upon him';

- receiving forgiveness: 'John appeared proclaiming a baptism of repentance for the forgiveness of sins'.

Of course, because Jesus' baptism was his first 'yes' to the cross, the revealing of his vocation to identify with sinful humanity so as to bring ultimate redemption and healing, the Easter imagery is still present, but not dominant. *Common Worship: Christian Initiation* includes full seasonal provision for Epiphany (pp. 150–55) and a new Vigil Service (see the outline order on pp. 132–3) incorporating Christian initiation. Many churches will want to use this provision and plan to have baptisms (and when possible, confirmation) on this day.

The Order for the Eucharist on the Festival of the Baptism of Christ makes provision for congregational renewal of baptismal commitment.

- After the Sermon, water is poured into the font with the words:

> God in Christ gives us water welling up for eternal life.
> With joy you will draw water from the wells of salvation.
> **Lord, give us water and we shall thirst no more.**

- The Epiphanytide Prayer over the Water from *Common Worship: Christian Initiation* follows.

- An acclamation drawn from Revelation 22 (the river of the water of life) may be used.

- An extended act of penitence and dedication may follow, including the following petitions:

> We have broken the pledges of our baptism,
> and failed to be your disciples.
> From all our sins, O Lord:
> **wash us, and we shall be clean.**
>
> We have shown indifference to those in need
> and have been afraid to stand up for justice and truth.
> From all our sins, O Lord:
> **wash us, and we shall be clean.**

- Water may then be sprinkled over the people, or they may sign themselves with the cross using water.

- The president says the Absolution, and the service continues with the Peace.

Where space allows, it is most effective if the congregation gathers around the font for this rite.

The extended Dismissal Rite includes an evocative responsory drawn from Byzantine sources and material in *Promise*:

> The Father's voice bears witness to the Son.
> **God has revealed himself to us.**
>
> The Son bows his head beneath the waters of baptism.
> **God has revealed himself to us.**
>
> Submitting to John's baptism, Christ delivers us from bondage.
> **God has revealed himself to us.**

A Service for the Festival of the Baptism of Christ

This is adapted from the famous 'Three wonders' service of *The Promise of His Glory*. It is an imaginative exploration of the 'three wonders' of the Epiphany: the coming of the Magi, the Baptism of the Lord, and the first miracle Christ wrought at Cana in Galilee. While the service is suggested for Epiphany 1, it may be used at any point in the Epiphany season. It is set out as a non-eucharistic service with the order:

• Magi

• Water into wine

• Baptism of Christ

Thus it culminates in the congregational renewal of baptismal promises. However, it can easily become eucharistic by changing the order so that the water into wine section leads seamlessly into the Liturgy of the Sacrament. In any case, the order will be partly determined by the geography of each church building and the position of crib, holy table and font.

> St Mark's is a large evangelical and charismatic church where the new rector is exploring how symbolism might enhance what had been quite a static approach to worship. He has started to use the large Victorian font at the west end of the building after years of using a small rose bowl at the front of the church for baptisms. The church had not had a crib, but on a parish visit to the Holy Land it was agreed to buy a beautiful set of olive wood figures. The rector looked at the service for the Baptism of Christ and was worried at first whether it felt a bit 'high church', and certainly any use of incense would be out of the question. However, after discussion with the worship committee, they decided to try it with the smaller and more creative Sunday evening congregation.
>
> The committee thought that the opening responsory was misleading (why 'this day'?), and so they agreed on the following order:

Welcome and introduction: we shall be exploring three great stories of the Epiphany.

Opening prayer.

Hymn: 'O worship the Lord in the beauty of holiness'

The congregation gathers at the crib.

Responsory

The figures of the Magi are placed in the crib.

Reading: Matthew 2.1–11

Short Address

Songs: 'Jesus, name above all names'
       'Immanuel, O Immanuel'
       'Like a candle-flame'

Open prayer

The congregation moves to the font.

Responsory

Water is poured into the font.

Reading: Mark 1.1–11

Responsive thanksgiving for water (omitting the formula of 'blessing')

Testimony by a new Christian

Songs, during which the members of the congregation are invited to wash their hands and faces in the water:
       'River, wash over me'
       'There is a river, whose streams make glad'
       'I'm accepted, I'm forgiven'

Open prayer

The congregation moves to the holy table and gathers around it.

Responsory

Bread and wine are placed on the table.

Reading: John 2.1–11

Short address

Songs: 'One shall tell another' ('Come on in and taste the new
    wine')
    'Seek ye the Lord all his people'

Eucharistic Prayer H

The Communion

After communion, prayer ministry

Final prayer and Blessing

Song: 'Rejoice! Rejoice, Christ is in you'

At the end of the service, members of the congregation
commented on how they had enjoyed using the whole of the
building and that the service was very worshipful. They saw the
three stories in a new light.

The case study illustrates how this kind of material can be used in a
formal setting, such as a cathedral or large parish church with a choral
foundation, or informally and very flexibly. Wise choice of music will
be an important element in successful use of this material. Where
church buildings are spacious, there is real scope for congregational
engagement through movement. If the crib is moveable, there is a
good case for placing it for this service so that the three 'stations' of
crib, altar and font have their own integrity.

The Eucharist on the Feast of the Presentation of Christ in the Temple

The Presentation or Candlemas is a Principal Holy Day in the
Common Worship calendar. Like the Epiphany, it may be celebrated on
the Sunday preceding 2 February if desired, and it marks the formal
end of the incarnational cycle. Indeed, it is truly a festival which looks
two ways: it points back to Christ's birth, but the searching prophecy
of Simeon – that Christ will be a sign to be rejected – also points
forward to his vocation to suffer and so, liturgically, to the nearness of
the season of Lent.

The following meditation, prepared for Durham Cathedral in 2005,
illustrates how many themes are reflected in Luke's profound narrative.

The Presentation of Christ in the Temple,

The Purification of St Mary the Virgin,

Candlemas.

Hypa-pante – The Meeting.

An ancient promise: The Lord whom you seek will suddenly
come to his Temple.
But who can abide the day of his coming?
Who can stand when he appears?
He is like a refiner's fire,
like fullers' soap.
He will draw near in judgement.

And the Lord comes: suddenly? In fire? In slaying judgement?

The Lord comes – as an infant, unremarkable, unrecognized,
gently, incognito.

God comes to his Temple – in lowly substance, in mortal flesh.
God presented to God, dedicated, consecrated, sanctified. God
given to God, given back, given away, given up. The Son of God,
given – with sacrifice; given first, as he will be given at the last –
the one true, pure, immortal sacrifice.

And the sign of this given life – two doves or two pigeons – small,
lowly, poor, understated – a small sacrifice for The Sacrifice, the
fulfilment of sacrifice, the end of sacrifice.

And Simeon, righteous, devout, aged, faithful, expectant, Spirit-
filled. A strange promise: you shall not taste death until you have
seen the Christ. Simeon, looking, longing, today and today and
today – perhaps today.

Spirit-led into the Temple – and there – with his eyes – he sees; he
sees what no-one else could see; he sees, he recognizes – in this
face, this infant, this child, tiny, weak, helpless, dependent,
innocent – he recognizes salvation, light, glory – no faded light, no
passing glory – light upon light, glory upon glory, for all people –
light for Gentiles, foreigners, the unclean, despised, forgotten,
irrelevant; glory for Israel – fulfilment, destiny, the end of
longings.

Now, at last, Sovereign Lord, Despotes, you dismiss your slave in
peace, faithful to your word, for my eyes have seen.

But then a blessing to amazed, speechless, puzzled, uncomprehending parents.

But no sweet blessing – to his Mother – now purified, cleansed, the destiny of this child, her child – to bring consolation, redemption, glory – the destiny – turbulence, division, contradiction, opposition, rejection, and a sword, sharp, excruciating, piercing, deep, piercing flesh, spirit, soul, piercing.

And Anna, aged, widowed, chaste, devout, intensely devout, ever-present, ascetic, prayerful, a prophetess – seeing the invisible – this child, this face – Anna the evangelist, the enthusiast, the missionary.

And us – tonight.

The Meeting – in word, in light, in Eucharist – the pure offering, the lowly offering – meeting us in sacramental gifts, silent, incognito, except for the eye of faith.

The Purification: cleansed – by fire, by light, by repentance, confession, absolution, by grace, by gift.

The Presentation – of ourselves, total self-offering, but in and with him, never without him. Presented again, given, consecrated, sanctified.

Candlemas – bearing Christ, Light, glory, light for all, glory for all – but perhaps with it a sword – a mixed blessing, a turning to Lent, to passion, the cross, the hard and narrow way – for the sake of the world and its salvation.

And finally, our Nunc dimittis – Sovereign Lord, your slave, whose eyes have seen, fulfilment, completion, satisfaction, contentment, peace. Peace.

For this reason, *Times and Seasons* has followed *The Promise of His Glory* in placing the Candlemas procession at the end of the eucharistic rite (p. 194), with the creative responsory which acts as the liturgical 'hinge' between the incarnational and paschal cycles of the Christian Year.

So the post-communion is ordered as follows:

• lighting of congregational candles

- procession to the font or church door or other suitable place, with singing of the Nunc dimittis or the use of a responsory based on the Nunc dimittis

- Concluding Responsory and dismissal

The concluding responsory runs:

Father, here we bring to an end our celebration
of the Saviour's birth.
Help us, in whom he has been born,
to live his life that has no end.

Here we have offered the Church's sacrifice of praise.
Help us, who have received the bread of life,
to be thankful for your gift.

Here we have rejoiced with faithful Simeon and Anna.
Help us, who have found the Lord in his temple,
to trust in your eternal promises.

Here we have greeted the light of the world.
Help us, who extinguish [*bear*] these candles,
never to forsake the light of Christ.

Here we stand near the place of baptism.
Help us, who are marked with the cross,
to share the Lord's death and resurrection.

Here we turn from Christ's birth to his passion.
Help us, for whom Lent is near,
to enter deeply into the Easter mystery.

Here we bless one another in your name.
Help us, who now go in peace,
to shine with your light in the world.
Thanks be to God.   Amen.

The ministers and people depart.

Those accustomed to this material in *Promise* will notice that the rubric directing the blowing out of candles after the words 'never to forsake the light of Christ' in the Final Responsory has been omitted. There was a strong plea in the Liturgical Commission that, as in baptism, we carry the light of Christ out of the church building into our daily Christian living. Local churches may decide to retain the *Promise* approach or not.

A shorter Alternative Candlemas Procession is also provided and an appendix includes directions and texts for the more traditional practice of having the procession at the beginning of the Eucharist or, alternatively, before the reading of the Gospel.

It has been rightly said that if there is a danger of overdoing the use of candles, at least on Candlemas we should have a clear conscience. As well as the provision of congregational candles for the procession, many church buildings will lend themselves to the extensive use of tea-lights, provided that sensible health and safety precautions are taken. Inexpensive butane-filled lighters, available from DIY and hardware stores, enable many tea-lights to be lit quickly and safely. Again, as with all festivals, there is opportunity here for genuine community preparation so that an exquisite theatre for worship is prepared. This truly is mission-shaped worship, when adorned by the clear communication of the excitement and challenge of the coming of Immanuel into the world.

6 Conclusion

This book began by talking about a banquet. But at what point does enrichment lead to indigestion? That is an important question and certainly no individual church could contemplate taking on board all the material in *Times and Seasons* and certainly not all at once! The phrase 'wise and discriminating choices' has been used in more than one publication.

However, experience suggests that many churches have found their regular worship to be enriched by seasonal service booklets or the projection of texts. It is when thoughtful and well chosen text is adorned with appropriate music and symbolism, and good and varied liturgical leadership, that the Christian Year becomes both dynamic and exciting.

Many congregations have come to expect, and value greatly, the great annual liturgies, whether in the Easter, Christmas, or Agricultural cycles, that enable festival to be truly festive, and so stand out from the rest of the year.

Moreover, Anglicans are perhaps learning, or beginning to learn, to harness and develop the creativity found in many Christian people. Developments in shared ministry mean that there are now opportunities for many lay people to contribute to the ordering of worship – it is no longer a merely clerical preserve, dependent upon the energy and creativity (or lack of it) of the incumbent.

The potential riches in *Times and Seasons* will be truly discovered only if Christian communities think and plan together and ask the question of *how* we shall celebrate these great truths, which stand at the heart of the Church's gospel. This requires good planning, good teaching, and all the resources of Bible and tradition. It means harnessing all the gifts of word and music, symbol and ceremonial, imagination and flair. It demands that we give as much attention to enactment as to text, and that the important theological truths embedded in the liturgy are explored and applied to active Christian discipleship. Then, indeed, the banquet of worship leads not to indigestion but to transformation, the making of a people truly for God's own possession, so that his salvation might reach to the ends of the earth.

Index

Absolutions, Christmas 82
acclamations
    All Saints' Day 28–9
    Baptism of Christ 110
    Christmas 83
    Church unity 105
    New Year 92
Advent
    carol services 63, 64–5, 72, 74, 76
    celebrating 2, 5–6, 18, 57–77
    celebration of Christmas in 74–6
    darkness to light imagery 57, 65, 76–7
    Jesse Tree 68, 74–6
    lectionary 59–62
    length 5, 19–20
    moods and themes 5, 57, 62
    as season of expectation and preparation
        57–9, 64
    seasonal material 62–4
    Service of the Word 63
    Sundays 5, 59–62, 68–71
    vigil service 72
Advent Antiphons 72–3
Advent Prose 57, 65, 73–4
Advent Sunday 63–4
Advent Wreath 64, 65–72, 76
    at Christmas 66, 67, 76, 89
    at Epiphany 99
    lighting 65, 76
    linking church and home 72
    origins 66
    prayers at 68–71
    Times and Seasons material 67–71
All Saints to Advent 3–5, 18, 19–56
    as baptismal season 43–4
    calendar and lectionary 20–24
    as kingdom season 19–20
    and mission of the Church 24
    seasonal material 24–6
All Saints' Day 3–4, 6, 26–44
    Eucharist 27–30
    and Fourth Sunday before Advent 21
    as Principal Feast 20, 26
    Service for the Eve 39–42
        with children 42–3

Service of Readings 39
Service of the Word 30–35
Sundays before Advent 21
Thanksgiving for the Holy Ones of God
    35–8, 40
and unity of the Church 26
All Saints' Sunday 21, 26
All Souls' Day 3–4, 6, 20, 44–52
    Eucharist 45–8
    as Lesser Festival 20–21, 44
    non-Eucharistic services 48–52
Alternative Service Book 1980 1, 14, 99
anamnesis (remembrance) 10
Annunciation to the Blessed Virgin 17, 95

baptism, renewal of promises 109–10, 111
Baptism of Christ 7, 99, 100, 101, 102
    Eucharist 109–10
    Service of the Word 111–13
Beatitudes 27
Benedictus 60, 87
Bidding Prayers
    Advent carol service 64
    Christmas carol service 87
Birth of John the Baptist 17, 95
Blessed Virgin Mary 8, 17, 95
Blessings 15
    Advent 63, 70–71
    All Saints to Advent 25–6
    All Saints' Day 29–30, 34
    Candlemas 102
    Christmas 83
    Church unity 105
    Epiphany 102
Bonar, Horatius 56
Book of Common Prayer 5, 7, 13, 98
Breaking of the Bread, Christmas 86

Call and Celebration 44
Candlemas 5, 6, 7–8, 11, 101
    Eucharist 113–17
    meditation 113–15
    as Principal Feast 113
    procession 16, 115–17
candles, congregational 76–7, 115–17

children
   and Advent 74–6
   and Advent Wreath 69
   and All Saints' Day 34–5
   confession 90
   and Eve of All Saints' Day 42–3
Christ the King 4–5, 20, 54–6
   and Initiation 44
   readings 23–4
   as Sunday before Advent 21
Christian Year
   enrichment 14–15
   rediscovery 2, 9, 13
Christingle service 74, 89
Christmas 6, 18, 78–97
   additional prayers 91
   carol services 74, 87–8
   celebrating in Advent 74–6
   crib 79, 84–5, 91
   crib service 89–91
   lectionary 81–2
   saints 17, 79, 94–6
   seasonal material 82–91
Christmas Day
   and Advent Wreath 66, 67, 76
   Eucharist 84–7
Christmas Eve 79
   crib service 84
   Eucharist 84–7
   intercessions 82
Christmas Tree 79–80
Collects, for All Saints' Day 33–4, 38
colour
   liturgical 20, 45, 58, 67, 76, 99
   in worship 2
Commemoration of the Faithful Departed
      3–4, 6, 44–52
   Eucharist 45–8
   non-Eucharistic services 48–52
Common Worship: Christian Initiation 43–4,
      73, 100–101, 102, 109
Common Worship: Daily Prayer 39, 63, 72
Common Worship: Festivals 14, 16–17, 62, 79,
      94–7, 101
Common Worship: Main Volume 15, 24–5,
      30–32
Common Worship: Pastoral Services 48, 49, 50
Common Worship: Times and Seasons 13–15
   Advent 62, 68
   All Saints to Advent 31–4, 45, 50, 52
   Baptism of Christ 115–17
   Christmas 78
   Epiphany 86, 100–106

confession
   and Church unity 102–3
   congregational 24
   invitations to 14, 15
      Advent 62
      All Saints to Advent 24
      All Saints' Day 31
      Baptism of Christ 101
      Christmas 82
      Epiphany 101
   for use with children 90
   see also Kyrie confessions
Conversion of Paul 17, 100–101
Covenant renewal 93–4
Crashaw, Richard 84
crib 84–5
   blessing 84, 91
   and Dismissal Gospel 86–7
   at Epiphany 99, 112–13
   and Magi 79, 108, 112
   prayers at 91
   and presentation of gifts 106–8
   procession to 84
crib service 89–91

Day of the Lord 6, 9–10
Didache 27, 63
dismissal Gospels 27–8
   Advent 64, 69
   All Saints' Day 29
   Christmas 81, 86–7
   Church unity 105
   mission of the Church 106
dismissals
   Advent 70–71
   Advent Sunday 63–4
   All Saints' Day 27, 28–30, 35
   Christ the King 56
   Christmas 86–7
   Church unity service 105
   Epiphany 106, 108, 110
   and mission of the Church 105–6
Doddridge, Philip (quoted) 58
Donne, John 6
Durham Cathedral
   Advent carol service 64–5
   Candlemas meditation 8, 113–15
   Christmas carol service 88

Easter Liturgy 16
Easter season 18, 78–9
Easter Sunday, and biblical time 9–10
Easter Vigil 10, 109

Egeria (early pilgrim) 6
Eliot, T. S. 6
Endings 15
    Advent 63
    All Saints to Advent 25
Enriching the Christian Year 1, 14, 15, 24–5
Epiphany
    as baptismal season 7, 109
    celebrating 6–7, 11, 18, 98–117
    and crib 99, 106–8, 113–14
    Eucharist 106–8
    and Magi 98, 113
    as manifesting glory 7, 98–9
    and mission 100, 105–6
    and presentation of gifts 106–8
    seasonal material 101–6
    Sundays of 99
    and unity 100, 102–5
eschatology
    and Advent 59, 63–4
    and anticipation of Advent 19, 21, 24, 55
    and sacred time 9–10
Eucharist
    All Saints' Day 24–6
    All Souls' Day 45–8
    Baptism of Christ 109–10
    Candlemas 113–17
    Christmas Night/Morning 84–7
    Epiphany 106–8
Eve of All Saints' Day 39–42
    with children 42–3
Evening Prayer, and Advent Antiphons 72

feasts, festivals and lesser festivals 9, 20–21
First Sunday in Advent, readings 59–60
flowers, in Advent and Lent 67, 80
font, and Baptism of Christ 111–12
four last things, and Advent 3, 19, 59
Fourth Sunday before Advent, readings 21–2
Fourth Sunday in Advent, readings 61–2

Gathering 16
    Christ the King 56
    Christmas Eve/Day 84
    Remembrance Sunday 53
Gaudete Sunday 67
Gloria in excelsis
    in Advent 58
    at Christmas 84
Good Friday, and biblical time 9–10
Gospel Acclamations 15
    Advent 62
    All Saints to Advent 24

Baptism of Christ 101
Candlemas 101
Christ the King 55
Christmas 82, 86
Epiphany 101
Greeting
    All Saints' Day 27, 31
    Christmas/Eve/Day 85

Halloween, as vigil of All Saints 39–43
'Hark, the glad sound!' 58, 75
'Hark, a thrilling voice is sounding' 58
Herrick, Robert (quoted) 78
'Hills of the North' 70
Holy Communion Order 1 16, 17
    for All Saints 27–30
    for All Souls 45
    for Christmas 84–7
Holy Cross Day 17, 44
Holy Family 81, 83
Holy Innocents 79, 94, 95–6
'How sweet the name of Jesus sounds' 96
hypapante (meeting) 5, 8, 114

initiation, at All Saintstide 43–4
intercessions 14, 15
    Advent 63
    All Saints to Advent 24–5
    All Saints' Day 32–3
    All Souls' Day 47–8
    Baptism of Christ 101
    Candlemas 101
    Christ the King 55
    Christmas 82
    Epiphany 101, 106, 108
    Holy Innocents 95–6
    for mission 101
    Naming and Circumcision of Jesus 96
    St John the Apostle 95
    St Stephen 94–5
invitations to communion, All Saints' Day 27

Jesse Tree 68, 74–6, 80, 99
John the Apostle and Evangelist 79, 94, 95
Joseph of Nazareth 17, 82, 95
judgement, and Advent season 3, 5, 55, 57, 58,
    60–61, 62, 64

kingdom season 19–20, 24
Kontakion for the Departed 46
Kyrie confessions 15
    Advent 62
    All Saints to Advent 24

Christ the King 55
Christmas 82
Epiphany 101, 106

Lacey, T. A. 72
lectionary 3, 26, 59, 81–2
Lent 18
and self-denial 2, 11
Lent, Holy Week and Easter 1, 14, 16, 27
light, at Christmas 80
Liturgical Commission 1, 14

Magi 7, 79, 98, 108, 112
Magnificat 61, 62, 87
Maranatha 5–6, 48, 63, 68–9
Marshall, Michael (quoted) 13
Mary Magdalene 17
Mason, John (quoted) 9
Maundy Thursday, footwashing 16
memorial services 48–52
Michael and All Angels 17
Milner-White, Eric 87, 88, 91
mission of the Church
and Advent 69
All Saints to Advent 24, 27–8
and Candlemas 117
and Epiphany 100, 105–6
movement, in worship 2

Naming and Circumcision of Jesus 79, 95,
96–7
Neale, J. M. 72
New Patterns for Worship 16, 63
All Saints to Advent 24, 25–6, 55
All Saints' Day 27, 31
Epiphany 102, 105, 106
mission of the Church 105–6
New Year 92
New Year
celebrating 6, 92–4
and Covenant renewal 93–4
Nunc dimittis 87, 108, 116

O Adonai 72, 74
'O come, O come, Emmanuel'
72, 73
O Emmanuel 72, 73
O Key of David 72, 73
O King of the Nations 72, 73
O Morning Star 72, 73
O Root of Jesse 72, 73
O Wisdom 72, 73
Odilo of Cluny 4

Palm Sunday 5, 6
procession of palms 16
Paschal Candle 6
Patterns for Worship 14, 15, 24
Peace, introductions to 14, 15
Advent 63
All Saints to Advent 25
Baptism of Christ 101
Candlemas 101
Christ the King 55
Christmas 83
Epiphany 101
Perham, Michael 1, 13, 14
'Phos hilaron' 39
Pius XI, Pope 4, 54–5
place, and Christian Year 2, 8–12
poetry, recovery 2
prayer for the departed 4, 44, 50
Prayer over the Water 109
prayers of penitence
Advent 71
All Saints' Day 31
Baptism of Christ 110
Christmas 84
and Church unity 103–4
Prefaces
Advent 63
All Saints to Advent 25
Christ the King 56
Christmas 83
for Church unity 104–5
Epiphany 102
extended 15, 26
mission of the Church 105
Naming and Circumcision of Jesus 96–7
St John the Apostle 95
short 15
Preparation of the Table, Prayers at 15
Advent 63
All Saints to Advent 25
All Saints' Day 27
Christ the King 56
Epiphany 101–2
Presentation of Christ in the Temple *see*
Candlemas
Presentation of the Four Texts 44
processions
Advent carol service 65
Candlemas 115–17
to crib 84
Epiphany 107–8
The Promise of His Glory 1, 14, 15–16, 19
Advent 64, 67–8, 72–3

All Saints to Advent 25, 27, 35–6, 39, 45, 52
  Baptism of Christ 111, 115, 116–17
  Candlemas 115, 116–17
  Christmas 80, 86, 91
  Epiphany 102, 111
  mission of the Church 105–6
  New Year 92
Purification of the Blessed Virgin Mary 7

readings
  Advent 64, 75
  All Saints to Advent 21–4, 26
  All Saints' Day 26, 32, 40–42
  Christ the King 56
  Christmas 81–2, 87–8
  Epiphany 102
real presence, in worship 10–11
Remembrance Sunday 4, 19, 20, 50, 52–4
  Act of Commitment 54
  ecumenical Order 24, 52–4
  and Third Sunday before Advent 21
renewal of baptismal promises 109–10, 111
responsories
  Advent carol service 65
  Advent Prose 73–4
  Candlemas 115–16
  Epiphany 110, 111–12
Rites on the Way 44

St Stephen, celebrating 79, 94
saints, Christmas saints 17, 79, 94–6
Scripture readings, short 2–3, 15–16
  Advent 64
  All Saints to Advent 26
  Baptism of Christ 102
  Christ the King 56
  Christmas 83
  Epiphany 102
seasons, resources for 14, 15–16
Second Sunday before Advent, readings 22–3
Second Sunday in Advent, readings 60
Service of Light 39–40

Service of the Word
  All Saints' Day 30–35
  All Souls' Day 48–52
  Baptism of Christ 111
services 15
Silk, David 24, 84, 87
A Song of the Holy City 42
sprinkling with water 104, 110
symbolism 118
  Advent 67–8, 74–6
  Christmas 79–80
  Epiphany 99, 111
  recovery 2

Te Deum Laudamus 40, 55
Thanksgiving, post-Initiation 44
Thanksgiving for the Holy Ones of God 35–8, 40
Third Sunday before Advent, readings 22
Third Sunday in Advent, readings 60–61
Thompson, Francis (quoted) 11
time
  and Christian Year 2, 6, 8–12
  and liturgy 10–12, 99
  and Two Ages 9–10
Together for a Season 72
Transfiguration of Our Lord 17

unity of the Church
  and All Saints 26
  and Epiphany 100, 102–5

Visitation of Mary to Elizabeth 17, 95

Watts, Isaac (quoted) 19
Week of Prayer for Christian Unity 100
Wesley, John 93
Wichern, Heinrich 66
worship
  as banquet 13–18, 118–19
  and lay creativity 118
  local needs 3, 15, 38

Lightning Source UK Ltd.
Milton Keynes UK
UKHW020637080720
366174UK00003B/211